PREPARE TO DEFEND YOURSELF

Prepare
to
Defend Yourself

COLIN OPIE

KINGSWAY PUBLICATIONS
EASTBOURNE

Printed in Great Britain for
KINGSWAY PUBLICATIONS LTD
Lottbridge Drove, Eastbourne, E. Sussex BN23 6NT by
Richard Clay Ltd, Bungay, Suffolk.
Typeset by Central Southern Typesetters,
Eastbourne, E. Sussex.

Contents

Preface

It could be said that the seeds for this book were sown about eighteen years ago. It was at this time that I was invited to a local judo club. When I joined, the dojo (training hall) was a small, almost derelict room on the upper level of a disused building in a bus depot. Somehow this did not seem to matter. The quality of the instruction, and the number of friends found, made visiting that little room a sheer delight. About a year after joining, we moved into a large wooden hut housing a mat that must have been at least twice the size of the old one. On reflection the new premises were not exactly Olympic standard, but at the time I remember thinking, 'Wow! This is it! What a joint!'

I stayed at this club until, in my middle teens, I developed a severe skin condition. When this condition was particularly bad, my parents bandaged the top half of my body each time I trained. I looked like an Egyptian mummy. But I did not want to cease training, for within a few weeks the area championships were to be held. It turned out to be a memorable weekend for me. First there were the South-western Junior Judo Championships of 1971. This was my last possible year of entry—and I came out with the gold for the under 60kg group. I remember pinning my opponent to the ground with a hold known as *yoko-shiho-gatame*. I poured all my experience of shifting weight and grip to keep him there. Those few seconds of the count-down seemed endless. Then the decision came—'*Ippon*'—I had done it. I leaped up in the air, not really thinking or caring what the judges thought.

The next day there was an area demonstration and a grading. Once again the 'mummy' went into action and proudly appeared at the end of the day with his next grade. Unfortunately the skin condition became worse and I soon had to give up training. It was not until my university days that I started training once more.

I tell you this for a number of reasons. Not least is the sense of immense satisfaction when you achieve something that you feel is worth while. I loved the sport of judo and it helped me to grow up fit and healthy. The controlled discipline of the training hall taught me to respect other people and not to be aggressive towards my peers. It gave me confidence in the school environment. I knew that I stood a chance of walking away from a fight before it even started if I simply refused to make the first move. If a school fighter decided he wanted to fight anyway, I knew I was still in with a chance to put him off before either of us got badly hurt.

Not once in all my days of judo did I find anything in the sport other than good things. No instructor ever talked about Zen philosophy, and I have no reason to believe that any of them practised Zen for themselves. I became a Christian in the years between giving up junior judo and going to university. At university I started judo training once more, this time as a Christian. I had no qualms about this. To me, judo was an exciting sport, pure and simple. It was only five years later, when my wife Jill and I moved to Watford, that I came across the notion that the martial arts were not good for Christians to learn.

I was seeking out a judo club, but failed to find one. One evening I walked into a sports centre and met a friend of mine who was a school teacher. It turned out that he was an aikido instructor, and a good one at that. Sensei Yates (*sensei* is the Japanese term for a martial arts instructor) was to become the principal British instructor for the British Yoshinkan Aikido Federation. A few minutes on the mat with him and I was hooked.

No literature existed on the martial arts and the Christian, so I followed my conscience carefully. I actually ended up training mainly at another club under the careful instruction of Sensei Thompson, who later became the chief instructor for the British Ken Shin Kai Aikido group. However, in neither club could I find any basis for the fears that some Christians held about the arts. From the first day I started aikido I talked to any and every instructor I could, and all of them knew me as a Christian. I learned at one point that Yu Sensei, an international instructor who had trained both Sensei Yates and Sensei Thompson, was himself a Christian. He was a Korean and had trained in Japan for many years. One day I had the privilege of meeting this man. All I wanted to talk about was aikido—after all, here was a man of exceptional talent, so why miss a good opportunity? But he flatly refused. 'I no want to talk aikido,' he said. 'You Christian. Tell me more what love is. Sometimes I no like student, he may be bad. I wrong? You tell me.'

The more I found out about the arts on a practical and purely factual basis, the more I felt that many of the criticisms aimed at them by Christians were unfounded. There are danger areas within most of the arts, but the boundaries are usually well defined. The Christian simply need not cross these boundaries.

Over the years my interests led me to the study of simple self-defence techniques. Here I found a certain element of what I can only describe as martial artists' élitism. By this I mean that self-defence techniques were largely based on one particular art, and that each instructor felt his art was the best. Mock combat situations could be demonstrated using very technical moves to fight off multiple attackers. This gives an unreal and unfortunate view of self-defence, unreal in that often the mock situations would be nothing like the real thing. For example, the attackers would usually know what was coming and would be defeated with an acting skill second to none. The view is unfortunate in that it gives people the impression that they have to be technically brilliant to survive. This puts off the people who most need self-defence.

There is no doubt that top-ranking martial artists are thoroughly competent. But even lower-grade black belts, if they are honest, would admit that they would not find such technical competence easy to sustain in a prolonged and truly aggressive attack. So if it is not easy for them, it is most certainly impossible for the average member of the public. What is needed is simple but effective self-defence techniques that are not geared to any one art. As far as self-defence is concerned, let us abandon élitism and give self-defence back to whoever requires it—whatever their natural abilities may be. We cannot afford to substitute what looks impressive for what will actually work for most people.

Knowing that the physical aspect of self-defence is only the last resort, I became interested in crime prevention techniques for the layman. My Christian outlook on life gave me a special concern for issues such as child abuse, abortion, and sexual harassment and assault. Self-defence can deal with all these things. Sometimes I think that *self*-defence is not the correct term. Perhaps it should be called *neighbour*-defence. It is a subject that causes us to become more aware of our surroundings and which creates a practical stimulus for the well-being of ourselves, our family and our neighbours. And we all know who our neighbours are—don't we (see Luke 10:29–37)?

For a number of years I have taken the self-defence workshop at the Royal Week Christian holiday held every summer in Cornwall. These workshops have given rise to many a stimulating conversation with other believers. Those who have attended the workshops, and more besides, have always approached me and asked the same question I had asked myself many years earlier: 'Is there a book that talks about Christians and their possible involvement with the martial arts or self-defence courses, and contains all or part of the material you are presenting here?' The response was always the same. I would say, 'No, I don't believe there is. I'm sorry.'

Well, now there is! Crime has always been with us. Our

response as Christians in dealing with this plague will differ widely—of that I am sure. This book does not, and could not, provide one simple answer for all Christians—a version of 'this is the way, walk ye in it'. It is really my apologia about being a Christian in the world of the martial arts.

One of my aims is to put the often exaggerated view of these arts into perspective and provide a dividing-line for involvement by the Christian. Self-defence is really about prevention. Physical defence is to be avoided at all costs. Having said this, preventioon does not imply total safety. Part 3 of this book is therefore devoted to a short but tried and effective course in physical self-defence techniques. Most books on self-defence will enter into varying degrees of detail about what to do when, concentrating on the physical aspects. Some of the better ones will include discussions on preventive measures, such as what locks to buy for your house and so on. I have not yet seen a book on self-defence covering rape trauma and the consequences of reporting a rape, or one that discusses child sexual abuse and how to detect and avoid it.

Another of my aims, therefore, is to provide a book for the Christian community that will fill the gaps. If you wish to read further in any particular area, I hope that any references I may give will be helpful. Where no explicit references exist, the intention is that you use the substance of what has been said to choose your next step wisely and with at least some pre-knowledge. Above all, I want this to be a book that will enable the whole family to work together for the common good and safety of all.

When discussing crimes I have only mentioned those things that are 'common to all men'. I leave it to you, the reader, to decide whether or not such things could happen to a Christian. I have also covered a broad spectrum of crime prevention measures. It is up to you to select which of these, if any, are worth pursuing.

Appendix 3 introduces a specialist group, known as the Martial Arts Fellowship, which operates under the umbrella of Christians in Sport. If you are a Christian and wish to take up a martial art or are already practising one, CISMAF would be pleased to hear from you. CISMAF may also be able to put you in touch with a Christian instructor for the purposes of learning simple self-defence.

Throughout the book I have tended to use the term 'he' when in fact either sex could be meant. This has been done simply to make the text more readable. I apologize to those who are offended by this. Any names of people used are purely fictitious, though their characters or experiences are real enough. Where a proper name has been used, it is by permission and for a special reason.

At certain points I have referred to what the law states about various issues. I am no expert on law, and would even hesitate to call myself a fair amateur. Even the most experienced judge cannot acquire complete knowledge of the law, for it is too large and indefinable a thing. But it is important to have some feeling for what the law states. A problem arises, however, in that the law is constantly changing. As far as possible I have endeavoured to state the law as it applied up to the end of April 1986. In any event, I have only stated the law as it applies to England and Wales. Scotland and Northern Ireland have their own laws, and obviously readers in other countries will be subject to different laws again. All I can suggest is that you read my comments, not for their absolute truth, but for their relative, informative nature.

In writing this book, I am indebted to all my past and present instructors in judo and the martial arts. Without them my skills and interest in crime prevention would not exist. Participants in the Royal Week 86 self-defence activity posed as models for the pictures shown in chapter 10 where Martin Harris has performed a stirling job in creating such good sketches from my rather mediocre photography. Thanks go to Paula Burley and Terry Irving for their support at Royal Week over a number of years. As a police officer and qualified karate instructor, Terry has made a number of contributions to the discussions on self-defence in this book, and has supplied me with detailed information regarding the training practices of European karateka. I am thankful to both him and his wife Sue for their continuing friendship.

Finally, but far from least, I acknowledge the part my wife Jill has played in all of this. She has spent much time making honest comments on the text, and has taken extra care of the everyday family needs so that I could devote time to writing. Her life is a sermon in action that I do not equal.

> But thou, O Lord, art enthroned for ever;
>   thy name endures to all generations.
>   (Psalm 102:12)

COLIN OPIE

PART 1

Facing the Issues

I
Should We? Would We?

It would not be impertinent to enquire about the validity of this book within the Christian family. Clearly I and other Christians associated with the production believe it has a place, or it would never have seen the light of day. But before jumping straight into a discussion on crime prevention and self-defence, it is important to understand the grounds for our conviction. It is also important to have a feeling for the limits of involvement that must be set, if the faith of the believer is not to be compromised in any way. Christians cannot simply pick up a few books on self-defence, or attend a martial arts club, and accept all that is encountered with gay abandon. Neither should they go to the other extreme and, by their actions, express a clear disregard for the safety of their family and neighbours.

At this stage I need to make one thing clear. When I speak of self-defence and crime prevention measures, I am including in this a host of related topics such as house insurance, places to avoid after dark, and a detailed knowledge of the area where you live. I am not simply referring to physical self-defence techniques. Also, let us face the facts about human nature in its current fallen state. Crimes have been committed, and man's inhumanity to man has existed, ever since Adam and Eve were banished from the Garden of Eden. As the band Dire Straits say in one of their songs, 'These things will always be the same, so why worry now?'

In response to this we must affirm first and foremost that it is not worry or anxiety that brings us to this point. Jesus himself clearly says, 'Therefore do not worry about tomorrow, for tomorrow will worry about itself' (Matthew 6:34). We arrive here simply through need. We need to know how we can be most effective within our own community to help combat crime and enable others to feel loved and cared for rather than bullied and frightened.

Secondly, things are not and will not always be the same, though society has been marred by violence throughout the ages. Man's defensive methods in Old Testament times were not as technically advanced as our microprocessor-controlled burglar alarm systems, but houses were still built to deter robbers. In Hosea's day there were even gangs of priests who were willing to murder and rob travellers along the highway (Hosea 6:9). However, the scale and severity of violence in our society is reaching epidemic proportions. Regard for human life is being reduced to naught. Policing strategies have been turned upside down in just a single decade. Today there are not enough policemen to protect everyone all the time, so the community as a whole must become involved. This is not to say that we can take the law into our own hands, but there are many Neighbourhood Watch schemes that enable every member of a neighbourhood, young or old, to feel that someone, somewhere, is looking out for them. Other options are also open to us.

As Christians, active social involvement does not, of course, preclude prayer—far from it. People that are starving to death in disaster areas need our prayers, but they cannot eat prayer. Elderly people who are afraid to go out need our prayers, but prayer will not transport them to their social event. Prayer is required when a neighbour is being attacked in an alley, but practical help (even if not physical inter- vention) may also be needed. The Christian faith demands that we have a keen social awareness. We cannot simply bury

our heads in the sand; indeed true prayer will always encourage us to keep our heads well up.

No doubt some would say that their faith is such that God
will be their sole protector. 'I have no need of self-defence,'
they declare. But is this faith? Where do you draw the line?
Would you stand by and let a member of your family be
beaten or raped? Do you say that there is no need to lock up
your car or your house? After all, you pray for a guardian
angel to be set over them each day, and you have sufficient
'faith' to believe the request has been granted.

What about house insurance? Would you say that this is a
waste of money and that prayer will keep away devastation
by fire, flood and burglary? And what of your unbelieving
neighbours and their safety? Do we always know which of
their anguished moments are direct acts of God, and which
are simply the result of living in this dangerous world? Of
course not! What we can be certain about is God's immense
love towards us his children (1 John 4:9–12), and his desire to
see all men saved and entering into a knowledge of the truth
(1 Timothy 2:4).

Do not misunderstand me. I am not saying that angels do
not exist, nor that we should be obsessed by protective
measures. I am simply making the plea that sensible action
should always accompany our prayers.

Faith in a sovereign Lord

In considering the Christian attitude to self-defence, we do
need to be clear about the true nature of biblical faith.
Christian faith is not a conviction that anything we ask of God
will be readily granted. Rather our faith is one that enables us
to believe and hope in the eternal promises of God whatever
our daily experiences may be.

One experience could be that of persecution, as illustrated
vividly in the great chapter on faith in Hebrews 11. In verse 36
we read about something Michael Baughen in his book *The
Prayer Principle* (Mowbray, 1981) calls 'disaster faith'.
Believers were jeered at, flogged, chained and put in prison,

stoned, and even sawn in two. Historical records give details of believers being lowered in nets as food for lions, and of being covered in tar and set alight at night to act as torches. All these things happened to them on account of their faith. They knew that God does not promise to take us out of the world, but simply to be with us in it. Their faith was an eternal one, a faith that looked forward to something far greater than mere temporal life on earth.

The death of loved ones is another experience we have to face. How many thousands of Christians were prayed for daily during the two great wars of this century, but died in battle or on home ground? More recently I heard about a group of young, dedicated Christian surgeons and doctors in Thailand that were suddenly killed along with their wives and children in a road accident. Such an incident gives us immense problems if we believe that God offers physical protection at all times and in all places.

In fairly short succession three of my dear brothers in Christ died, two of them relatively slowly of cancer, one very quickly and unexpectedly of malaria. I still become a little tearful when I think of these men. All three loved the Lord and were strong pillars in their own sphere of ministry.

Why? How can these things happen? There are no easy answers, and much greater minds than mine are unable to comprehend the sovereignty of God and the mystery of suffering. But our faith is in this God. A faith that does not assume that we will be free of all ills, but that we are victors in Christ Jesus whatever may happen.

Applying our faith

If, then, Christians live in the same fallen world as everyone else, and are open to the same dangers and perils, why bother to learn about crime prevention and self-defence?

I suggest that it is simply because we are talking about two entirely different sources of suffering. Suffering through persecution for righteousness' sake, and suffering through natural disasters, are both true tests of faith. On the other hand, suffering an attacker's onslaught for no other reason than his wont and pleasure, has little or nothing to do with faith. Rather it has everything to do with the violation of someone's civil liberty.

One thing is certain: we do not learn about self-defence in order to ward off any and every aggressive intrusion. Suppose we lived in a country that banned Christian activities of any kind. One day a knock comes on the door and we are confronted by two men who say we are to be arrested because we were known to be holding a (supposedly) secret meeting. Should we use our knowledge of physical self-defence techniques to prevent the men from arresting us, and then try to escape the authorities in some way? I suggest not. After all, reasonable precautions were taken. The meeting was intended to be a secret one, but somehow the authorities found out. What is more, we were caught in the building and in the act. This is now our opportunity to put our faith into practice, and to trust God regardless of what may happen.

By contrast, if we were walking back to our house and we saw the men before they saw us, it might not be a bad idea to turn round and praise God for his protection over us.

If we analyse our responses to different situations, we will find that things are not as black and white as we may first have thought. Let me illustrate this point by a story related to me by a dear Polish brother.

He was in a Siberian camp during the last war. Conditions were unbelievably harsh. At times it was so cold that a man's ear would freeze solid and fall off. A soldier came up to a group of prisoners who were chopping down trees in the intense cold. The soldier asked if any of them knew how to construct a brick furnace, because a new hut was to have a number of such furnaces built into it. In desperation the Polish Christian said that he knew how to do it. He said this not because he did know, but because it would give him a chance to get inside. But what was he to do now? The next day he was to start work on the furnaces. If the soldiers found out that he had lied, it would almost certainly mean death or a very severe punishment. That night he prayed that God would help him, and God did so in a miraculous way. While he slept, he had a dream. The dream was a complete blueprint for the design of a brick furnace!

We could argue from this that our brother should not have lied in the first place. But he did, and God still came to his aid. We could put the lie to one side and say that this whole episode was one of God's signs of love and care towards his children. Personally, knowing how God has used this man since the war, I am glad that God mercifully spared his life during those horrific years in Siberia. I also know that this brother spent much time sharing his faith with other prisoners. At one point the camp commandant threatened to kill him if he did not stop this 'propaganda'. Our brother replied, 'Yes, this you can do, but no more!' Such was his faith.

The way in which we interpret and apply our faith will differ between Christians, and may even alter personally depending on the situation in which we find ourselves. We must accept these differences if we are to avoid tearing one another down and so destroying the house that God is building. But whatever position we adopt, may it be one that combines reasonable practical activity with undying faith.

Prayer and practicalities

This leads us on to the wider issue of the social cancer of crime. How should we view our involvement here? If we have a serious illness we will pray. We will also listen to what the doctors prescribe, take the necessary medicines and carry out any precautionary measures. In all of this we will seek God for his guidance and help. So it is with the illness of our society. We should pray both for God's intervention and for our own safety and that of our relatives and neighbours. We should listen to what the crime prevention and defence instructors prescribe. We should take the necessary precautions to try and alleviate, and if possible eradicate the pain and distress.

But how many of us do this? With apologies to Mark 10:

25, 'It is easier for a whale to pass through the laser hole of a video diskette than to convince Christians of their ability to aid crime prevention.' Of course, physical and mental make-up will condition our response to this as individual believers. But some response, no matter how small, would be preferable to total disbelief and apathy. From experience I would say that greater emphasis should be laid on self-defence. Too many people are afflicted with the 'it won't happen to me' syndrome. If they bother to think about it, they may also be unsure about what their response would be if they came across someone else being attacked. Without some form of guidance and training, the chances are that they would do the same as any other person—react on the spur of the moment. This could turn out to be fatal for more than one party.

The golden rule of love

The gospel writer John made an important and fundamental statement of truth when he said: 'This is how we know what love is: Jesus Christ laid down his life for us. And we ought to lay down our lives for our brothers . . . Dear children, let us not love with words or tongue but with actions and in truth' (1 John 3:16, 18).

It is impossible for us to love our brothers and our neighbours in the way God intended unless we first have his Spirit within us. We must be sure, then, that we really are members of God's family. An outcome of becoming a child of God is that our hearts and minds are renewed and we are increasingly aware that we should help and comfort, as far as we are able, anyone who might cross our path. But if we are truly to share God's love with others, it is essential that we first have some appreciation of just how much he does love us. Different people grasp the depth of God's love in different ways. For me it is the fact that God sent his only Son. Would I give up my son as a ransom for the lives of other people? I doubt it very much. Yet this was the depth of God's love, that he sent us his Son, and his Son willingly gave up his life for us.

Even when Christians do have a clear understanding of

God's love towards mankind, love does not necessarily come easily to us just because we are believers. We are far from perfect and are more than capable of making errors. Moreover, the chances of making such errors are more acute when it is our immediate family that is in danger. Let us assume that the fictitious Christians in the following stories have had no training at all in crime prevention measures or simple self-defence techniques. They are, however, committed Christians and we can assume that prayer is an integral part of their reaction. Also, they are well aware of the commandment to love one's enemies.

Mandy wakes up in the middle of the night and hears a burglar downstairs. Her husband is away on business. There is no telephone upstairs, and she has two young children in a room across the landing. What should she do?

Karen, a mother of two teenage boys, lives in the inner city. While walking home late one night she sees a gang of youths ahead of her. For some reason she feels threatened, as though she knows they are going to attack her. In what ways can she react so as to defuse the situation?

Martin has gone fishing with his young daughter Kate. They have chosen a nice quiet spot in the highlands. Kate wanders off a short distance to watch a butterfly she had just noticed. Suddenly there is a scream, and on turning round, Martin sees a heavily built man attacking Kate. There is no one else there but them. Martin's natural instinct is to rush towards Kate and help her. Instead of running off, Kate's attacker draws a long knife from his back pocket. It is as if Martin's feelings about what is happening have blunted his senses, and he lunges into the attacker with all the strength he can muster. In the ensuing moments the knife is accidently bent back towards the attacker and he is killed. How will Martin feel? Was he right, both legally and morally, to react in this way?

At this point, do not suppose that I am going to give you all the answers. Nobody can do this for you. In theory we cannot afford to overreact. But without some training, I dare to suggest that this is what most Christians would do. I do not mean by this that they would deliberately overreact. Love must envelope both the attacker and the person being attacked. Do not fall into the trap of thinking that this is an easily learned skill, or something that is endowed by God on the day of our conversion. But take comfort in the fact that our Father realizes this, even when we forget it.

The subject of loving our enemies is brought right to the fore when studying the Sermon on the Mount. We will look at this Sermon more closely in the next chapter, but for now let us assume that there is no excuse for not trying to live up to the high standards found within it. After all, Jesus lived by such standards and he has sent the Spirit to empower us. We must keep our hearts free from resentment, revenge and anger, no matter how badly we are treated. Over and above this, we must seek the good of those who are abusing us.

Although we will never be able to do this perfectly, we can come some way towards it by striving and grace. Surely Jesus would not have suggested it, if he knew we could not even aim for it—and Jesus was talking about the here and now, not eternity. This golden rule of honesty, sincerity and love must prevail in our lives. It must be seen to be at work in everything we do.

Civil liberty and justice

Christian love does not exempt us from civil involvement. 1 Peter 2:13–17 and Romans 13:1–7 state that the courts of law have been ordained by God as a controlling influence on society, and as such we should be subject to them. The criminal element in society must be met by justice. Forgiveness does not imply lack of justice. The two must co-exist.

A convicted prisoner who truly comes to believe in the Lord during his sentence should not attempt to negotiate a reduction in his time. (He cannot normally do less than a third of his time anyway. A third can disappear through parole, and another third through remission, but that is all.) The prisoner has met with forgiveness from the supreme court of God, but justice for the crime must still be applied. He knows, perhaps better than most, that the rest of his time is really a suffering for justice's sake. Although forgiven, he knows he deserves his allotted punishment.

Our Christian faith should not be an excuse for refusing a specific role in civil or national defence. There is no reason why God's kingdom cannot exist within another one. Indeed, until the Last Day it is hard to imagine our existence in any other way. Matthew 22:21 clearly shows God's kingdom existing within the kingdom of Roman rule. In Acts 10 we read of the first gentile convert—a Roman centurion. This centurion was not asked to cease being a soldier—he was simply commanded to be baptized.

Consider the Christian policeman. In his life as a whole he will endeavour to follow the teachings of Jesus. When he is on duty, he must apply the regulations for the administration of criminal justice. This is his duty, and it is right for him as a Christian to carry out that duty. Under certain circumstances it may be possible for him, or the authorities to which he must answer, to exercise mercy to some degree or other. But if not, justice must be administered according to the law of the land. To have no criminal law at all would give rise to anarchy. Robbery, murder, rape, kidnapping, terrorism and all other social offences would simply take over, and society as we know it would collapse. I fancy that this is at least one of the reasons why God, in his mercy, ordained the existence of governments in the first place. This is very much a part of his grace, even though theologians call it 'common grace'.

National defence and pacifism

Similar arguments could be applied to the armed forces. Space does not permit a detailed discussion of the use of weapons here, and I fancy we would all disagree somewhere along the line anyway, but I will state my own convictions over this matter. I do believe in the deterrent value of the armed forces, and I do believe being a member of the armed forces is an honourable occupation for a Christian (provided he has a suitable physical and mental make-up).

The fact that we Christians abhor war and desire to see it abolished completely, is no excuse for us to sit back and allow others to fight for our liberty (or our neighbour's). Jesus commends putting our own life in jeopardy rather than allowing others to suffer. In John 15:12–14 he says that we should love one another as he has loved us. Jesus laid down his life for us ('we' being referred to as 'friends') and said that 'greater love has no man than this, that a man lay down his life for his friends'.

If you say that you are a Christian and a confirmed pacifist and that you refuse to fight or defend yourself, then I cannot say you are wrong. I cannot judge you and say that your faith is no faith at all. What I will say is that I am doubtful that such a stance by a Christian is commendable. However, I know that feelings run hot over this issue, and it is important that we make our own decisions before God in coming to our final position.

The real-fruit yoghurt syndrome

Taking any stance in personal, civil or national defence measures is fairly easy in theory. But what about in practice? Are we sometimes like a yoghurt purporting to be of a particular 'real-fruit' variety, when in reality we are full of nothing more than artificial substitutes? The trouble is we will probably never know until our theory has to be translated into action in a moment of conflict.

A person trained in self-defence could freeze solid when under attack and become totally passive. A soldier may not be able, when faced with another pulsating human being, to squeeze the trigger. The pacifist, when put to the test, may be unable to stand by and allow an act of inhumanity to occur. All these things are possible. Statistically, however, it is much more likely that a trained person will react positively, according to his background. A moment of conflict will create an almost, if not total, automatic response. There is nothing mystical or odd about this—an appropriate automatic response will be supplied by anyone under given conditions, peaceful or hazardous. Take an experienced carpenter. Talk to him about anything and, while talking, hand him some nails. Keep talking and see what he does with the nails. Whatever he does, it will be a much more ordered and subconscious act than any similar activity carried out by a non-carpenter.

The point is this. If we desire to be 'real-fruit yoghurts', we must be as sure as possible that we know how far we would go, and that we could accept before God any likely consequences. For example, suppose you are a woman who wants to learn effective self-defence. If a given type of attack required you to grasp a man's genitals as part of the defence, would you be able, mentally, to do it? If you were being attacked by a man with an axe in his hand, could you bring yourself to strike him in the solar plexus hard enough to severely wind him? (Compared with some American articles these two examples are 'mild' responses.) And then, would you be willing to go the extra mile and ensure that an attacker accidently injured by you received the appropriate medical treatment through some appropriate means? These questions, and others besides, will continually rear their heads throughout the following chapters. In the majority of cases it will be up to you to answer them, in so far as you can before being placed in the situation itself.

I have no doubt that experience, together with the passing of the years, will alter our opinions about topics of applied morality (i.e. not basic Christian doctrine, but issues facing a current society). In this sense we cannot be too emphatic about our current feelings. We must allow ourselves room for manoeuvre and accept that other members of God's family may hold entirely different views.

2

The Sermon on the Mount

Within a lifetime of service for the King, the average Christian will hear a great many sermons. But however great the preacher, and however instructive and eloquent his delivery, no sermon can better the sermon on the mount for the very heart of Jesus' teaching. And this sermon is particularly relevant to our current discussion.

The importance of Matthew's account is shown by two major facts. First, it is placed very near the beginning of the New Testament. Secondly, it is known that early Christian writers used quotations from this gospel more than the other three. Within the gospel account itself, Matthew seems to place a great emphasis on recording this sermon of Jesus (it is irrelevant to us here whether the recorded sermon was given in a single hearing or not). Historical records give good reason to suggest that the sermon was given around the same time as the choosing of the twelve disciples. It had taken about one-and-a-half years, since the beginning of Jesus' Galilean ministry, to make this choice. Matthew's view of the importance of the sermon is shown, therefore, in the fact that he records it in his gospel before going on to record the Galilean ministry itself.

If the early church took such notice of this sermon, then we should sit up and take notice as well. But before we look at the relevant sections, let me reiterate an important point. When I use the terms self-defence and crime prevention, I do so only as a type of shorthand. I am not referring simply to the physical combative element of self-defence, for to do this would be to emphasize what is by far the smallest element. It is also the element which should only ever be used when all other defensive measures are precluded. Conversely, I do include in the term anything that enables us to be effective and loving guardians of our families, our neighbours and, finally, ourselves.

The Beatitudes (Matthew 5:3–12)

Those who share the dispensationalists' view might consider the Beatitudes to be a kind of New Testament parallel to the Law of Moses. They would stress the conditional nature of the proclamations: if you want to be blessed, then be a peacemaker, have a pure heart, be merciful, and so on. Furthermore, there is an implication in this interpretation that if, for example, you are not a peacemaker, then you are not blessed and neither shall you be a son of God. This could have an extremely negative effect on us. Fear and legalism could easily creep into our lives. We could misinterpret the way of the peacemaker and adopt a totally passive acceptance of any external evil influence.

But this is not what the Beatitudes are really saying. They are more a statement of fact about Christian lifestyle. We are the humble in spirit. We are the peacemakers. We are the merciful. We are those who are persecuted for righteousness' sake. Our blessedness is in the fact that this is our state of being as Christians. This blessedness is clearly not created by the conditions themselves. The Beatitudes are not new laws which leave us feeling bound and oppressed. Rather they show us our status before the Father on account of our new life in Christ. With this in mind we can take positive steps to be the most contrite, merciful and righteous peacemakers the world will ever know. It is not surprising, then, that the

Beatitudes come very early on in the New Testament, for the spiritual stance they describe is essential before we can tread the path of discipleship that Christ marks out later. Self-defence is not incompatible with living out this glorious state of being to the full. We progress from being an indecisive bystander of today's problems to a preserver of standards and a helpmeet to our neighbours.

Salt and light (Matthew 5:13–16)

These two terms are best interpreted as referring to a 'preservative' and a 'guide'. We know that while the world's moral standards decline and shift, God's standards remain constant. It is one of our responsibilities as Christians to try and preserve God's standards within our nation. For our part, this comes about in two stages of activity, in addition to prayer.

First, we will endeavour by our words and actions to guide people to the one true Light—Jesus Christ (John 8:12). Having been used by God in this way, we will go on to nurture and strengthen these new believers. Note here that our light is not our good works themselves, but the way in which these good works reflect the nature of our God.

Being a preserver and a guide has many practical facets, as well as spiritual ones. In both the physical and spiritual dimensions we should seek to use our gifts to the best effect, including our knowledge of self-defence. It is another aspect of being a useful and caring member of the community. It does not imply that we can walk free of all evil, take the law into our own hands, or become neighbourhood vigilantes. Neither does it permit us to justify a huge and disproportionate insurance cover, or break all an attacker's limbs before telling him God loves him!

Murder versus anger (Matthew 5:21–26)

There are two passages in the sermon on the mount that are going to be a problem to Christians right up to the Last Day.

One of these concerns the sixth commandment, 'You shall not kill' (Deuteronomy 5:17). Jesus goes even further and says that we should not even be angry with our brother. This brings us face to face with both physical and mental conflict. The other passage is found in Matthew 5:38–42, and we shall look at this later.

The sixth commandment relates directly to the physical element found in self-defence measures, and it poses an important question. In so far as physical self-defence is based on the martial arts, why be trained to the point where we know how to hurt, maim or kill someone if we are specifically commanded not to do so? This must be answered realistically. First, let us look at the context of the passage.

The Jews clearly thought that murder was defined by the overt act, and it was this act that would be tried in the local Jewish court. The judgement referred to in Matthew 5:21 is that of the local court. Jesus, as we know, goes further than this. He tells the people that the intention behind murder should also be tried in the court (or the local church, as it was to become for the Christian), whether or not the act is committed. It is a parallel to the passage in verses 27-28 about adultery. It is not only the act that is sinful, but the intention behind it.

We also know that Jesus makes two further comments about crimes of even greater severity than anger. Whoever insults his brother is also liable to judgement. Traditionally this insult was achieved by saying to a person 'raca', which means 'empty head'. This was a denial of that person's self-respect, and an admission that you considered that person to be of less importance than yourself, almost to the point of being worthless. Such a crime should be brought before the Sanhedrin—the supreme court. The court was to pronounce judgement on a person found guilty of such injustice to a fellow man. The insult 'you fool' had the implication of 'godless man'. This was an even worse insult than 'raca', and was to be regarded as one person denying the moral standing of another before God. Clearly, no man is able to judge the standing of another before God (Matthew 7:1). This insult would be judged by the heavenly court—the only court qualified to make the correct judgement.

So we find that not only murder is sin, but also anger and abusive language. You may say, 'But I do not swear, I have never uttered a bad word since the day the Lord came into my heart.' Well, you may be right—for the moment. Have you ever been angry? Husbands, have you ever come home from a bad day at work and bombarded your family with your anger as soon as one foot is over the doorstep? Drivers, have you ever wanted to get out of your car and verbally abuse the 'maniac' who has just pulled out in front of you? If you can honestly say that you have never sworn or been angry, then either you are quite unique or you need to study 1 John 1:8 right now!

It is quite possible for us to fall into these sins. That is why the sermon on the mount—the very heart of Jesus's teaching—is so hard to follow. In the light of this, I find great comfort in 1 John 1:9—'If we confess our sins, he is faithful and just, and will forgive our sins and cleanse us from all unrighteousness.'

A Christian leader once discovered this ability to fall into sin with some embarrassment. He was trying to fix his car. This man happens to be active in the ministries of teaching and preaching, and has held numerous key positions of responsibility for the spiritual well-being of many Christians. His own daily walk with God is an example to us all. As all you mechanics know, fixing a car sometimes has its problems. This brother was trying desperately, as I remember it, to undo a nut. The nut would not budge. Suddenly the spanner slipped and he hit his hand hard against the engine. He swore. His son, who was watching closely (and no doubt advising as well), suddenly rushed into the house shouting, 'Daddy swore, Daddy swore!' To make matters worse, they happened to be visiting some friends at the time. A number of relatives and friends arrived at the front door and just looked at him. What could he say except sorry? He just stood there and apologized while his son was busy shouting, 'Say it again Dad, say it again!'

This leads us on to a further and most important point. We know that it is possible to fall into these sins, and we know that Jesus forgives sin. However, this does not give us a licence to accept failure. The context of 1 John 1 should be noted. Here, John was countering gnosticism, the belief that the spirit is good, but matter is evil. This philosophy gave people the freedom to practise all manner of sin, while concurrently assuming they had a pure spirit. John's message is clear. We must confess, 'agree with God about', the sins that are knowingly in our lives. If we object that we do not sin when, by comparing our lives with Scripture we clearly are sinning, then we make God out to be a liar. John's intentions are even clearer when he says that he wrote his letter so that his readers may be free from sin (1 John 2:1).

Although it is neither common nor desirable for us as Christians to sin, we must recognize that the possibility is there. John Wesley wrote in 1761, 'After the heart is cleansed from pride, anger and desire, it may suffer them to re-enter. . . .I cannot perceive any state mentioned in Scripture from which we may not (in measure at least) fall.' It took Wesley some time to reach this conclusion, because he wrote this some twenty years after first preaching his famous sermon on perfection.

But why am I labouring this point? What significance has it for us today? It is simply this: however pure and holy we may be today, there are instances in our lives that, for a brief moment, will cause us to fall. Imagine returning home and finding your spouse being attacked. How would you react? Suppose you are walking up an alley one night and an attacker suddenly confronts you? How would you feel? Or maybe you are walking home one day and spot an older boy beating up your son. How would you deal with the situation? I dare say that many of us would react on instinct, simply because that is all we have to fall back on. But your emotions could take over, you could end up using force when it is not needed, or more force than is required. Anger could creep in and destroy the response a Christian should strive to achieve. We cannot afford to overreact. An attacker is human, and God loves him as much as you or anyone else he is attacking.

This takes us back to the original question, 'Why be trained to the point where we know how to hurt, maim or kill someone if we are specifically commanded not to do so?' The paradox is that by knowing how to do these things, we become acutely aware of how fragile the human body is, and we will know what to avoid doing. An inexperienced defender may simply lash out in desperation, producing a totally uncontrolled strike. A knowledgeable defender will be aware of non-fatal defence tactics and will be careful to avoid performing, as far as his attacker allows him, any truly harmful technique. In essence, the trained person will at least be relatively calm and controlled in his response.

Revenge (Matthew 5:38–42)

These five verses are probably the most widely misconstrued in the whole of the sermon on the mount. On a first reading, they give enough ammunition to would-be fanatics to start up entirely new sects. Did Jesus really mean that in all circumstances we are to allow our offender to beat us to a pulp or rape us? Are we to give to any who ask, regardless of our own situation and whether or not we have the means? Are we to offer to stay with our captors once our use has been fulfilled and our freedom is set before us? By no means!

The term 'eye for an eye' is a reference to Exodus 21:22–25. It relates to the punishment for a man who strikes a woman who is pregnant, accidentally or not. Different rules apply for injury or death caused simply by men fighting. This context shows that Jesus is not concerned here with the legislation of the courts. He is much more concerned about how individuals should treat one another—that is, without revenge.

The beatitude about being 'persecuted for righteousness' sake' is applicable here. In cases where the glory and knowledge of God will be exalted, and our own righteousness tested and refined, the options are clear—we should suffer gladly the loss of goods, or physical abuse. As verse 39 puts it, we 'do not resist'. But the whole context of this is in not seeking justice for ourselves. Rather, we are to love our enemies, feed them and generally supply their needs (Romans 12:19–21). Vengeance belongs to God, and God alone.

There is no suggestion, however, that by silence or inaction we should encourage injustice to ourselves or others. People are constantly being mistreated, not for righteousness' sake (many are not even Christians), but for the sheer enjoyment of the perpetrator of the crime. There is a world of difference between being persecuted (mentally, verbally or physically) because of a righteous stand that we take, and a sporadic attack made upon us by some other person. I would further suggest that our active response to a sporadic attack is independent of whether or not the attack is because we are Christians. For example, I would still defend my wife if a Satanist was about to stab her ceremonially on account of her beliefs. If, however, I was on an inner-city street mission and the person I was talking to was about to punch me in the face because he didn't like being called a sinner, I may well ignore my training. There may be, as we shall see in later chapters, other reasons why we may decide not to intervene (at least regarding a personal attack). But these reasons cannot be deduced solely from a reading of Matthew 5:39.

Even if we decide not to resist in a physical way, we can still turn to the heavenly court. For there is no suggestion in this passage that we may not resist the works of evil men through prayer and supplication. Our response should always be a positive, active one, and never a passive one. This is where 'turning the other cheek' applies itself. If an attacker confronts me with a spiked knuckleduster in his hand, I would be very unwise to allow him to make the first strike, let alone the second. Under such circumstances the choice of permitting a second strike would not be mine to make. If, however, a man insults me and slaps my face in the age-old way, I am under instructions to turn the other cheek. His blow was, of course, a challenge, rather like 'throwing down the gauntlet', and I am not allowed to rise to that challenge. In both cases my response is an active one. In neither case does an expression of vengeance or anger exist. The purpose of each response has been to defuse the violence within the situation.

Turning the other cheek has other implications in our modern society. Take my knuckleduster-clad 'friend' as an example. No benefit would have been gained for me or him or society at large if I had simply allowed him to carry out his attack. If by words or actions I am able to defuse the situation then some benefit will have been achieved. If I am then able to share my faith with the attacker, even greater benefit will have been accomplished. Suppose the attacker is very aggressive, so that words fail and a physical response is required. This response could be anything from running away for help to immobilizing and restraining him. If he is arrested by virtue of my actions, my response can continue. I can take an interest in what is happening to him if, for example, he ends up on remand.

A remand prisoner (i.e. an unconvicted prisoner who is awaiting trial) has many more privileges than a convicted prisoner. These privileges, which are little more than normal operational procedures, are laid down in the 1964 Prison Rules. In particular, remand prisoners may send and receive as many letters as they like. They are also usually allowed one visit per day, so I could make contact with him if I really wanted to. I can do my best to make it clear to him that no anger or revenge is in my heart, and that God loves him. My concern may fall on a stony heart, but on the other hand it may not. Apart from God, who knows what effect a sown seed will have?

In addition, my feelings towards similar people must remain pure. If it was a man dressed in a studded leather jacket who attacked me, I must be careful not to let this prejudice me against all men dressed this way. Each person I meet must be treated on his own merits. I must make no assumptions about people on account of their speech, clothing or the colour of their skin. Above all, I must remember what Jesus says about forgiveness in Matthew 18:21–22.

Walking the extra mile and giving freely to people in need (Matthew 5:41–42) are the means by which we can exercise this positive response to injustice. The constraining and visiting of the prisoner described above is an example of going that bit further. There are other ways too. In New Testament times people would have readily understood what Jesus was saying here. Officials were perfectly within their rights to demand a person to carry their gear for one mile—it was a form of slavery. We should not think that they were showing how righteous they were by going the extra mile, nor that the official should particularly notice their love for him. By going the extra mile they were effectively relieving the next person of the burden. In this they were showing their love and concern for their neighbours.

True riches and anxiety (Matthew 6:19–21, 25–34)

This passage of Scripture gives good advice on a basic crime-prevention measure. The context does not suggest this, but the effects are the same. Jesus was concerned about those who would compromise their faith and consequently become anxious. He drew the attention of his hearers to the collection and use of riches, pointing out that 'no one can serve two masters' (Matthew 6:24). The emphasis was not on riches being evil in themselves, but rather the motives behind the creation and amassing of such riches.

A basic question we must ask ourselves is, 'Do we desire material wealth to the point where we cannot let it go?' A well-known comedian highlighted this in one of his sketches. A mugger came up to him and said, 'Your money or your life.' A moment passed and the comedian made no reply. Becoming impatient at the delay the mugger reiterated, 'OK, come on, what is it to be, your money or your life?' The comedian frowned a little and replied, 'Wait a minute will you, I'm thinking.' There is no need to think. We all live in temporary accommodation. Why try to grasp on to that which we cannot keep? Are not our treasures in heaven far greater?

There is a very sensible rule in self-defence that says if a mugger just wants your money, then give it to him. If a burglar just wants the hi-fi, let him have it. What is it to you?

If a mugger grabs a woman's handbag, she might well hold on and refuse to let it go, but in so doing she is in danger of increasing the violence of the attack. The same goes for men who are approached by muggers, but refuse to hand over their wallets. What do you have in your possession that is worth fighting or dying for? Do you carry large sums of cash around with you? If so, I strongly suggest you change your habits.

I am not advocating here that Christians should get rid of all their riches. In today's modern society there are any number of reasons why expensive items may be owned by Christians. The professional photographer needs some very expensive equipment. The freelance computer consultant may have a powerful computer system at home in order to help him in his work. The professional musician may well have a very old and valuable instrument. It is important that these items are owned, and sensibly protected and insured. For all the passages in the Authorized Version that mislead through using language that is now outdated, the rendering 'take no thought' (Matthew 6:25) must be one of the most unfortunate ones. The original Greek does not mean this, and believers who use it as a basis for a denial of responsibility are much mistaken. The passage is speaking about over-anxiety and attachment, not thoughtful precautions.

How do we achieve a balanced attitude to possessions? We are all different, and what seems reasonable to one may seem unreasonable to another. There really is no simple answer. We must follow our own consciences and at least consider the arguments brought before us by other Christians who are close to us. In addition to this, we must consider the practical implications of what we are doing. Are we leaving ourselves open to crime because of our folly? Are we misusing or over-protecting the wealth that God has given to us, instead of managing it to his glory? If, after all reasonable precautions have been taken, we are still anxious about the safety of our wealth, we have gone much too far. This aspect of self-defence should be one of the least to present any kind of problem at all to the Christian.

The conclusion of the sermon (Matthew 7)

The essence of this great sermon is in the relationships it endeavours to cultivate between individuals. Love is paramount, and we must exercise it in any and every way possible. But this does not preclude the necessity for civil justice. In Matthew 7:1 we read that we must not judge. However, as we have seen, this does not mean that we are never to exercise judgement over men who commit crimes. Neither does it mean that we cannot reach a judgement over fellow believers who have strayed from the truth. In the time to come we are to take counsel over angels (1 Corinthians 6:1–7), so we had better get some practice in now! Clearly it would not be possible to obtain discipline in the church if we were not able to exercise judgement.

What this verse does teach us is that we cannot stand aloof from the judgements we pronounce. We must be prepared to be subject to the same decisions. In Romans 13:1–7 we read that civil courts are appointed by God and we ought to be subject to them. There will also be times when it would be right and just to make recourse to these courts in order to deal with certain matters that affect the whole of society.

As an aside, it is worth noting the use of the word 'hypocrite' in Matthew 7:5. In the whole New Testament, this particular word is used only by Jesus. We must be aware that Jesus' knowledge of men's hearts was and is far greater than ours. I suggest, therefore, that we ought to be very wary about using this word ourselves—not least because in applying it to someone else, we are in all probability pronouncing a judgement that applies to us as well. You see, the word hypocrite does not refer to a person who is bad but is pretending to be good. It refers to a person who is so convinced he is right that he cannot be wrong. Could this be the state of our hearts as we pronounce judgement?

These things have important bearings on the subject of self-defence and crime prevention. While clinging on to the rule of love, we must still exercise judgement over wrongdoers. In exercising this judgement, we must be sure that we would accept the same judgement if it was to be pronounced over us. Some people believe that capital punishment should be brought back. If so, they must be sure that they would believe this no matter who was in the dock. Matthew 7:12 states this quite plainly: 'Whatever you wish that men would do to you, do so to them.' If you would expect a member of the public to come to your aid if you were being attacked, then you must also be sure you would go to their aid in some way.

Above all, remember that the hearers of this sermon were totally amazed at the end of it (Matthew 7:28). The scribes and Pharisees would teach the people from the law and the prophets. They would pass on the knowledge of their own minutiae that governed conduct. But they could not teach as Jesus taught—with first-hand authority. It is all the more important, therefore, that we take heed.

This book has been written within the bounds of this great sermon. To a certain extent, the understanding of what is written here is dependent on the correct interpretation of Scripture and a proper grasp of what I am really trying to say. I do not want any believer's faith to be compromised. At the same time I want the family of God to face up to, in a practical manner, the acts of crime prevalent in today's society. There are things we cannot do, and there are things we can do—each one according to the gifts and abilities available to us. May God give us the grace to do this with love and understanding.

3
The Way of the Martial Arts

In today's electronic village we are bombarded by the sensational: the story that will sell, the pictures that are designed to remain firmly fixed in our memories. It is a feature of the competitive age in which we live. As Christians, we are not immune to such clever marketing strategies. Slick salesmanship is no less used when advertising the feats of the martial arts.

We can see both the benefits and the dangers when we understand a subject in some depth, but often only see the dangers when we are unsure of the facts. We would be sensible to delay our judgement until we know the full facts about a particular subject. This does not, however, license the believer to make unfounded allegations. Let me illustrate.

Carl and his friend James both attend the same fellowship. They are young teenagers who love the Lord Jesus, and they both have Christian parents. They watched the Olympic judo championships on television and became interested in taking up the sport. They decided that they would go together, so as not to feel uncomfortable in an established club. Carl asks his father, an ex-marine, who thinks it would be a great idea. He could drop the boys off at the club and pick them up later. James' father is not so keen. He has read that judo is a martial art, the same as any other, and that it has oriental religious elements within its teachings. He is rightly concerned for the spiritual well-being of his son, and in a loving manner tells James that he cannot go. The result of it all is that neither Carl nor James takes up the sport. Furthermore, they become unsure about whether or not judo is a bad thing for Christians to get involved in. Their respective fathers simply agree to disagree. Would it not have been more prudent for both parents to visit a local club, talk with the instructors, see the club in action, and then make a decision?

Mike Taylor in his booklet *Martial Arts—Are They Harmless?* (Diasozo Trust, 1982) has made some good points about terminology used in the martial arts. He has also listed a number of important criteria to check for when making a decision about joining a self-defence class. Unfortunately he has grouped all the martial arts, including judo, together. No account has been taken of differences in training methods between the East and the West, and the whole text is based on research into articles and books. No attempt seems to have been made to contact registered clubs and talk with the instructors, or to contact the appropriate governing bodies. His resultant opinion is that all the martial arts (as taught in Europe and the USA) have an occult influence.

However, he does make an important point about feats performed by high-grade oriental masters. Feats are sometimes performed that would appear to have a mystical element, inasmuch as we cannot see how they could possibly be performed on a purely physical basis. The trouble is, many of us are totally unqualified to say whether there is a physical, psychological or spiritual factor behind the effect or not.

Aikido is one martial art renowned for being controversial in this area. Thomas Makiyama, a highly qualified eighth dan in yoshinkan aikido, has pointed out in his book *Keijutsukai Aikido—Japanese Art of Self-defence* (Ohara Publications, 1983):

There were those who attempted to convey aikido techniques through an alleged Zen-like philosophy, accompanied by stunts that incorporated elementary physics and common sense. These advocates insisted that a mysterious source of spiritual strength must be mastered (according to their teachings, of course) in order for one to learn the intricate principles of aikido. This is erroneous.

There are two points which we must consider in connection with this. First, there are many instructors like Sensei Makiyama that have a profoundly practical basis for their excellent display of technique. These instructors have been in the game for a very long time. They know, better than most people, about the bogus elements of past and present teachings. It must be assumed that the very early development of the martial arts in China was affected in some way by the philosophy of their creators. But this in no way implies that such interpretations or philosophical practices are required by the modern-day exponent.

Secondly, in the Western world we are unlikely to come across such remarkable demonstrations. If we should get the opportunity to see a respected master at play, we would certainly be in no position to make a quick and purely visual analysis of his techniques. The only thing we would know for certain is that the exponent has been practising for a considerable number of years, and for a considerable number of hours per day over this period. It is no exaggeration to say that a full-time martial artist is likely to take just one year to practise for as many hours as a dedicated westerner training for six to eight years. (This assumes that the westerner has a normal daytime job, and that he trains on average three nights a week.) Imagine taking two exponents who have each trained for six years, one exponent having been taught full time by top Japanese instructors, and the other having trained in the West as hard as possible, taking into account other commitments. Is it any wonder that we would be stunned at the technical excellence of one over the other?

The martial arts and martial ways

An important distinction exists between the terms 'martial arts' and 'martial ways'. Most literature does not make this distinction clear, but it has a vital bearing on how the Christian is to view the current situation.

An original Japanese term for what are commonly called the martial arts is *bujutsu*. *Bu* can be translated as 'military', and *jutsu* as 'art' or 'practice'. At this point, there are no spiritual or philosophical connotations to the term. We arrive at the phrase 'martial arts' by means of direct translation only. These military arts were, in the first instance, plain methods of defence and attack used within very real combat situations. If you did not know how to fight, you were dead. The choice was really rather simple.

It must be remembered that up to the 1860s and the start of the Meiji period of 1868–1912 (see Appendix 2), Japan was a feudal society. From the dawn of its history Japan had a class-based society with an emperor at the top of the ladder. As time went by, the emperors had less of a say in the running of the land, and by the twelfth century the shoguns held control. In terms of social order there were the shoguns, the daimyo (nobles), the bushi (knights), the farmers, and then the artisans and merchants. The servant class of the bushi, the samurai (meaning 'servant'), became the policemen of the era and held numerous privileges. In return for this status they owed total allegiance to their noble lords. In a feudal society this clearly implied a fight to the death if this was required. So we come back to the original point. If you did not know how to fight, you were dead.

Buddhism, mainly in the form of the Mahayana branch (the liberal branch of Buddhism emphasizing Buddha's spirit), entered Japan around the seventh century. In 741 A.D. it became the state religion of Japan. Zen Buddhism was fathered by Bodhidharma in China in the early part of the sixth century. As it started to wane in China around the thirteenth century, it started to make an impact in Japan. The important point to note is that the fighting arts, prevalent in Japan during its feudal periods, were known and practised long before the Zen philosophy arrived. In addition to this, Zen philosophy did not start to make a significant impact on the martial arts scene until the emergence of the Meiji period in the nineteenth century. It was at this time that the arts were studied less for their practical application, and more emphasis was placed on the philosophical elements.

To mark this shift in emphasis, the term 'jutsu' was replaced by 'do', meaning 'way' in the Zen philosophical sense of enlightenment. As modified forms of the arts arrived in the late nineteenth century and early twentieth century, each art of practice form became a 'way' form. The efforts of Dr Jigoro Kano turned jujutsu (pronounced 'jujitsu' and in feudal days also known as taijitsu or yawara) into judo. Morihei Ueshiba developed aikido from the ancient art of daito aikijutsu. Similarly, kyujutsu (archery) became kyudo, kenjutsu became kendo, and so on. In short, martial arts became martial ways.

Once again, it is clear from this history that the fighting methods of the Japanese bushi existed in a 'practice' (jutsu) form long before the Zen philosophy arrived. This means that Zen, as such, is not a requirement for gaining knowledge about the physical aspects of any martial form. Neither is Zen required to make you into a more successful exponent.

This is all fine in theory, but what about modern European clubs? Do they force students to practice Zen?

The prevalence of Zen in the martial arts

The fact that we still call the martial disciplines 'arts', and not 'ways', is significant. First of all, let us take judo. Judo is an internationally recognized sport and is included in the Olympics. In Britain judo is governed largely by the British Judo Association (BJA). The British Judo Council (BJC) has a smaller following. Judo is not in any way governed by the Martial Arts Commission (MAC), which was set up in 1977. As such we can freely say that as far as Britain is concerned, judo is a sport—it is not classified as a martial art. In 1983 the BJA saw a review of Mike Taylor's book mentioned earlier. In a personal letter from the then General Secretary of the BJA, I received this comment:

Judo has long since distanced itself from martial arts because we consider ourself to be purely a sport. The British Judo Association instructors pass through a graduated coaching scheme in order to become qualified, and this has nothing to do with any so-called occult practice.

In summary, therefore, the official position of this organization is to disregard such an article and in no way to associate ourselves with its content.

In the same year, the MAC also saw a review of the booklet and I received this comment from their General Secretary:

The philosophies have been rather neglected in twentieth-century Britain with its 5,000 clubs and 72,500 practitioners. I have taught the martial arts for twenty years and know all the senior British instructors. As such, I can confirm that occult practice is certainly not a part of their discipline.

It would be true to say that there are instructors in Europe and the USA who do practise Zen to one degree or another. But two points must be noted here. First, Zen is a most undefinable philosophy. Try talking to a Zen master and you are likely to be more confused at the end than you were to start with. And that is only if the master bothers to say anything. He could just as easily stick his finger in the air, throw a lotus blossom at your feet, kick a ball, or slap you in the face (see *Those Curious Cults* (Pivot, 1975) by William Peterson).

Those instructors who do practise Zen meditation do so for what they believe to be character-building qualities. The emphasis is not on perfecting a martial technique, but on perfecting themselves. Zen is as good a vehicle as any for 'inward improvements' of this kind. But Zen is incompatible with Christianity. Zen has no God, no future abode, and no soul to worry about. Zen meditation is supposed to improve the character of the practitioner by disciplining the mind. But philosophically Zen does not address matters such as good and evil, life and death. As Christians we have a distinctly different set of values. We cannot improve ourselves for we are a fallen race. Only Jesus can create in us a new heart. We must be born again through the power of God's Holy Spirit if we are ever to return to the kind of being that our Father intended us to be.

The message is clear. If an instructor tells you that Zen is necessary for improving your art, he is misleading you. What he means is that he wants to see an improvement in you yourself. Hopefully he would not even suggest it to you, as your Christian lifestyle ought to make him sit up and think anyway. He may consider on watching you that you already practise Zen! What a glorious opportunity to let him know otherwise.

Secondly, what of the trend in the popularity of Zen? Zen started in China around 1,500 years ago. It lost its popularity there in the thirteenth century, while gaining popularity in Japan. But Zen practices have waned in Japan in this century, while having caught on in the USA and, to a lesser degree, in Europe. How long will it be before Zen gets replaced by some other philosphy? Praise God that though all else changes, his word endures for ever!

The concept of *ki*

Some explanation of the term *ki* or *chi* is needed because it is very often confused and merged with the arguments about Zen in the martial arts. It is cited as an inner power that can be sent from the tanden—a point about 3 inches below the navel, or sometimes cited as a point behind or just above the navel— to any part of the body at will. The directed power of your ki will enable you to execute perfect technique and control your adversary with ease. Once again, problems over this arise from a misunderstanding of the oriental's way of thinking and the effect that his philosophies have on his thought processes. Before discussing this further, I want to state quite clearly that ki is not a power that overtakes you, it is not a demonic influence, and it is not a substitute for practice.

Perhaps the term 'ki' is found more in certain schools of aikido than in any other martial art. Note that it is only in certain schools. Aikido is split broadly into two schools: the 'hard' schools based on the Yoshinkan style of training, and the 'soft' schools based on the modern Uyeshiba system (headed by Kishomaru Uyeshiba, the son of aikido's founder). The soft schools are, in general, proponents of the ki principle, and certain schools place considerable stress on it. The hard schools do not advocate the ki principle in the same way and little attention is paid to its description. Other arts, such as karate, have senior exponents that make reference to ki. There is absolutely no doubt that some high-grade instructors use the term in a deliberately mystical way simply as an advancement to their own ends. The problem is, it does fool people.

A visitor once came to my club, and he stayed and watched until the end of the session. Afterwards he approached me and asked about a certain technique which the hard schools of aikido call *nikajo*, and the soft schools *nikyo*. Basically, he was sceptical that it would work. I showed him how to do it and invited him to apply the technique on me. He did—but to no effect. This seemed to support his theory. I then asked if I might try the same thing on him. He foolishly accepted and within two seconds he was on his knees pleading with me to let him go (which I did). This upset his theory a little, and he suggested that the only reason it worked for me was that I had ki and he didn't, or at least he didn't know how to get his ki 'flowing', as he put it. I do not know how he came to be aware of this terminology, but I suspect it was by reading some book, such as *What is Aikido* by Sensei Tohei, or a magazine.

At this point I have two options. Either I can tell him he is right and that if he pays me a princely sum per hour for the next six months, I will teach him all he needs to know. (This is easy because if he fails to achieve anything I can simply tell him that he is not concentrating sufficiently.) The other option is for me to own up to the fact that I have been doing the art for a considerably longer period of time than he, and what does he expect? My technique is bound to be better than his.

We are treading on very insecure ground if we start to think of ki as a dormant power within us, simply waiting to be trained. Morihei Uyeshiba, the founder of modern aikido, has emphasized the development of ki in terms of non-resistance. Ki, then, becomes the technique or principle of using mental concentration and physical movement in complete unison. With practice one can bring an attacker under control using a minimum amount of energy and the least possible force. The result of this should be to bypass any harm to oneself, while simultaneously inflicting a minimum amount of harm to the adversary. This at the end of the day is not a bad principle for the Christian to follow, and actually keeps him within the bounds of the law of the land.

Gozo Shioda, the only student of Morihei Uyeshiba officially graded to ninth dan, uses the word ki in his book *Dynamic Aikido* (Kodansha International, 1977) very sparingly indeed, but his treatise of the principle is plain. Spherical movements are emphasized, as are exceptional speed, precise timing, and concentration of power (known as *shuchu-ryoku*). Spherical movements are to embody the correct use of centripetal and centrifugal forces. Speed is used in two ways: one way is to keep up with an opponent, and the other is simply to avoid him. Timing is related to synchronization, and is a combination of speed and shuchu-ryoku. It has been said that timing is the ability to judge the exact moment a wave starts to turn back after hitting a rock. Although shuchu-ryoku (the concentration of all of your power at a given point in a specific instance) is not completely possible, regular training can improve one's ability enormously.

Ki is not some supernatural force, then, that enables you to do these things. It is a response that comes about by training, more training, and then more training. Because of the way the term has been misused over the past fifty years, particularly by westerners, I feel it is better not to mention it at all. A student is capable of performing a given technique, at a particular level of skill, according to the amount of practice he has put in. It is as simple as that.

It is fair to say that the centrality theme of the ki principle is of prime importance. A human body that is finely balanced at the centre of its lower trunk, and has its centre of gravity as close to the floor as possible, is many times more powerful than if out of balance and rising upwards. By way of example, consider the lifting of a heavy load. To lift the load with arms outstretched and a bent back will prove impossible. What is more, you are very likely to damage your back. If, however, you get alongside the load, bend your knees, and lift with a straight back using the power of your whole body as you push with your legs, you are very likely to succeed. Even if you do not, because the load really is too heavy, no harm will have been done.

Like Zen, ki is hard to describe. It is a term alien to our culture and language. Above all, we must not be misled by profit-seeking and egocentric practitioners. It is simply a word that attempts to describe the fulfilment of perfect technique, perfectly executed. A state of complete blending with an attacker. As Christians we may feel that we cannot train at certain clubs because the emphasis on the ki principle is too strong. The solution is simple—do not train at them. The proportion of martial arts clubs (taking all arts into account) that openly discuss and explain the execution of techniques in terms of the ki principle is very small indeed. The number of clubs that actually fully understand what they are talking about must be even less.

The tanden or lower abdomen

Earlier I mentioned that ki is often cited as coming from what the Japanese call the tanden. This region of the body is that which lies behind the navel. Sometimes it is referred to as lying a few inches below the navel. Its exact positioning is almost irrelevant for a number of reasons.

Any top Japanese instructor in, say, karate, judo or aikido will emphasize the point that your whole body must be used to execute a technique. The restricted use of just an arm or a leg will result in a weak execution of any particular movement. Any good sports coach will tell you the same. Have you ever seen a swimmer simply use his arms and leave the rest of his body limp? How many times have coaches used expressions like, 'Get your hips into it'? The simple fact is that when a human is standing erect, the centre of gravity of the body will be found in this area of the lower abdomen. As we are all slightly different in build there will be slight variations in the exact position, but the general region will still be behind the navel.

The concentration of power that we talked about when discussing ki can, it is true, be thought of as arising from the tanden. But this is nothing more than a physiological necessity for effective technique. The muscles in the lower abdomen are very powerful but slow to move. Also, they do not cause a great deal of body or limb movement. The muscles at the extremities of the body are weak but fast. By bringing the pelvic region into play first, and then transferring this muscular movement (and hence force) to the appropriate limb for the technique, maximum power can be brought into play. In other words, the greater the number of muscles that can be brought into use during the execution of a technique, the more effective the technique will be. In karate this 'whole body' principle can produce spectacular blows. In aikido the principle gives rise to a stable and unified body that can make an attacker think he has just walked into a brick wall, tried to bend an arm made out of cast iron, or been effortlessly thrown by some form of mechanical grabber!

Do not fall into the trap of thinking that either ki or its assumed source, the tanden, are in any way mystical. I repeat the words and thoughts of many top instructors in many arts when I say that there are laws of physics and pure physiological facts that explain their emphasis in the arts. Most sports also stress the 'whole body' principle (for this is where ki essentially displays itself). It is simply that sports which have no particular background in Japanese or Chinese culture use terms more familiar to us. Once again, it is only profit or status-seeking instructors of the martial arts who would dare to mystify oriental terminology.

Calmness of mind

Before finishing this appraisal of the martial arts, let me mention one other point, that of calmness of mind. Any good martial arts club will endeavour to instil, through practice, a state of relaxation in their members. This is yet another term that has been misconstrued as something spiritual, when it most certainly is not.

The type of relaxation, or calmness of mind, that is to be fostered is not a detachment from reality. It is what the Japanese call *zanshin,* and it is better translated as 'awareness'. It is the sort of awareness you would hope to find in a player if you were a manager of a football club. You would not want a midfield player that became rigid with indecision the moment he came into contact with the ball. On the contrary, you would like to see him capturing a bird's-eye view of the pitch, analysing the situation rapidly, and acting accordingly to his team's best advantage. So it is with the martial arts exponent. After long years of training, an instructor would expect to see a calm, composed and alert student in the middle of a free-style attack practice.

This principle of calm approach has important consequences. A body can only react at speed when it is relaxed. You can try this for yourself. Hold a hand out in front of you, about chest height and 6 inches away. First, tense your bent arm and fist as hard as possible, and then punch out straight as fast as you can. How did it feel? Did it seem very fast? Did it seem powerful? Now try the same operation with your fingers open loosely and with a very relaxed arm. This second attempt should feel faster and more powerful. The tension in your arm the first time actually delayed your movement. Fear makes us tense up physically. In this state, we either slow up or freeze altogether. Alternatively, we could become aggressive and put ourselves in even more danger.

It is not the clubs that advocate relaxed techniques that should be avoided. Rather it is those clubs that implicitly or explicitly provoke tense, angry and aggressive attitudes. More will be said about this required calmness when discussing the use of force in self-defence measures in chapter 9.

Practising a martial art

All that has been said so far relates, of course, to the Christian interested in taking up a martial art. If we take the number of practising exponents as a percentage against population, and apply that same percentage against the Christian population, the number of Christians likely to be thus interested is quite small. I could not even guess at absolute numbers. Suffice it to say I believe I am now relating to a small minority.

The first question you should ask yourself is, 'why do I want to learn a martial art?' If it is for self-defence, the remaining two parts of this book are more relevant to you. Martial arts clubs are generally only interested in teaching the intricacies of their art. They are not there to teach you self-defence. This is not to say that the physical aspect of self-defence will not be picked up as a by-product. It is simply that this is not the major concern of your instructor.

Is it because you want to improve your health or your posture? If so, why not take up swimming or aerobics, or both? It is because you are a shy person, and you want to build up your confidence in public? Well, there are services you can perform in your church that will help you, or maybe a hobby that will bring you into contact with new people.

I may seem to be contradicting myself here. First of all it appears that I am in favour of Christians practising a martial art, and then I think of a million and one reasons why you need not bother. But in actual fact there is no contradiction. The emphasis in this chapter has not been to excite Christian involvement in the martial arts. It has simply been a Christian instructor's analysis of the arts, based on experience in judo, aikido and traditional weaponry. It is important only that you know what the limits are, and what the necessary ingredients of any instruction should be. Beyond this, perhaps the only reason for practising a martial art is because you want to. You may want to keep fit, but you do not enjoy jogging and you detest water. Personally, I practise the martial arts for fitness. I do it because it is this that I have truly enjoyed and progressed in. I do it because I know that, as in our Christian experience, I will never attain absolute perfection in it—there will always be that challenging next step; I can keep on learning. In the long term, of course, there is one other facet. Being an instructor enables me to help others feel safer and become more aware of their surroundings, while instilling a spirit of non-violence on their part.

Playing with the martial arts

Practising a martial art is, under good instruction, a worthwhile activity should you wish to participate. Playing with the arts is quite another matter. While discussing 'murder versus anger' in the last chapter, I mentioned that by knowing the body's weak points we become better equipped to avoid hitting such areas. The converse is also true. Ignorance of weak points can be a danger.

It is for this reason that I would warn parents to guard against their children playing around, imitating their latest kung fu idol. I am not being a kill-joy here, and neither am I saying that children's rough and tumbles are not purposeful. But playing with martial arts movements is playing with fire. Arms and legs fly wildly with no genuine control. When I see children playing at being Bruce Lee or the Karate Kid, one or more of them frequently ends up getting hurt. Do you realize how easy it is for a wild kick to brush a knee-cap out to the side? Or that a child's breathing can be stopped by accidentally hitting his solar plexus with the heal of a shoe?

Such playing can also breed a desire to try out newly seen moves on their friends, with possible serious injuries to one or more children. You are probably aware of how easy it is for a child to get into the habit of gently thumping someone when a joke is made or whatever. If uncorrected, a child will carry this habit through to late teens and even adulthood. Now imagine that it is not a simple thump but a chop to the ribs or kidneys that the child is giving. One day the 'play' will not seem so funny.

The martial arts are a skill to be learned and kept to oneself, unless instructing other club members or under imminent life-threatening danger. They are too powerful to be played with, either by club members who know a little of what they are doing, or by film-watchers! Neither should *gi's* (practice clothing) be worn around the streets of our towns. Such behaviour invites bravado and entices certain members of society to edge the wearer into showing his skills, possibly by means of a fight. It is not customary in this country to wear such clothing in the open, so why do it? It is easy to put a track-suit over the top of practice clothing when travelling, breaking for lunch and so on.

I would be most encouraged if I never saw a move being practised or played with out in the open simply for fun. Clearly I do not include organized demonstrations here, or the open-air practices arranged on club nights or during national courses. What I am stressing is decorum, modesty and humility within a practitioner's lifestyle, and a cessation of dangerous play by film-watchers who have no idea what they are playing at. Perhaps when this happens the martial arts will gain a great deal more respect from the general public.

PART 2

Self-Defence Measures

4

Knowing Your Attacker

It is not possible to explain the definitive actions of each and every type of attacker. Although assailants can be split into a number of wide-ranging groups, no two people are ever the same. Your attacker may be a non-professional mugger or he may be a terrorist, but no two muggers or terrorists have the same physical and emotional make-up. Nor do criminals go around with badges declaring, 'I am an aggressive non-professional,' or, 'I am a sadistic terrorist,' or, 'I only want your money.'

The overall effects of a crime on a victim differ according to various types of attackers. For example, a rapist may say that he is not going to hurt you provided you co-operate. After the attack you realize that on a purely physical level the man was telling the truth. He was not the 'woman-hater' type of rapist, sadistic by nature and definitely out to hurt his victim. But after this crime of violence has been committed, it may take years of your Christian family life to reach the point where you can receive God's healing. Years of tears, torn feelings, utter rejection of your husband's affections, disbelief in what has happened and maybe even in God himself. Is this 'hurt' or not? Just how 'violent' was the crime?

The fact of the matter is that there is only one set of rules we can follow, regardless of the type of our attacker. So why am I bothering to discuss the issue of knowing your attacker? First, because we will be better able to understand why certain things can be done, either to prevent a crime taking place or to minimize the violence within a crime. Conversely, we will understand why there are other things that we must not do. Secondly, it will help to reinforce one of the basic truths of self-defence: a baby rattlesnake will kill you just as dead as a daddy one. Armed with this understanding, we can approach the practical material in the next chapter with a little more confidence that the suggestions given will help.

Types of attackers

Not all attackers or criminals are motivated in the same way. Some will never attack their victims armed, knowing that their punishment, if caught, will be more severe. Some will always attack with a weapon in their hand, but would never have the nerve to use it. Some will be highly organized in their attack, picking their victims very carefully. Some will attack totally at random. Without going into deep psychological explanations for this (which I would be totally unqualified to do), let us consider the more generally accepted types of attacker.

The circumstantial robber

This person is no mean, hardened criminal. His situation dictates that money must be obtained other than by legitimate methods. He may be on drugs and need the cash for his next 'fix'. His victims are not carefully picked out, and all things being equal, he will not be violent. However, he may resort to violence if you are too slow in responding to his requests or if something happens to make him panic. Remember, he is not a hardened criminal and he does not make a practice of robbing. There is every chance that he will be as nervous, if not more so, than you.

The professional mugger

In the main, this attacker has the same aims as the circumstantial robber. He wants your money and he wants to get away. However, he is a professional. You were picked by choice and the venue for the attack was also well planned. As such, you are at much more of a disadvantage. Once again, violence will generally only occur for one of two reasons. Either he is not getting what he has asked for quickly enough, or his ability to get away with the attack is under threat. An additional danger is, of course, that he may be the type to dispose of any witnesses to the incident, namely you!

The aggressive attacker

With this type of attacker, physical self-defence techniques will almost certainly be required if you are going to attempt to escape relatively unharmed. Although he may ask for your money, his real intention is that of harming you or abusing you as much as he wants. He does not usually understand why he physically assaults his victims, it is simply a part of his crime. This type of attacker should never be allowed to tie you up or cover your eyes under the pretence of only wanting something else, such as your money or your household goods. Sharon Tate fell victim to this approach and she and her guests were slaughtered by the Manson gang.

There is some sense in looking for the word 'only' in an attacker's speech in order to determine his possible aggressiveness. Suppose you are faced with a non-aggressive mugger or rapist (i.e. an attacker that will not become violent unless threatened). If such an attacker wants to rob or rape you, he will often make this plain without referring to the act as being the 'only' thing he wants to do. This approach is not infallible because an aggressive attacker can calmly make one assault after another with no warning at all. No amount of reasoning will help you with this type of attacker. If his intentions have always been to hurt you, that is what he will ultimately attempt to do.

The status seeker

There seems to be a new breed of aggressive attacker that does not fit into any rational group. I say this because their actions appear to be totally irrational. I refer to those who would, for example, walk up to someone, stab them and then walk away laughing. They are not after money, they do not seem to hold any grudge against the type of person attacked, and they have no psychological bent towards aggression. They may go around in gangs of between two and six members, or they may go it alone.

The disturbing aspect of this type of attack is that there is little or no warning. They may even walk past you quite peacefully before sending the Stanley knife across the side of your neck. I can only assume that this is due to some form of status seeking. The attacker will be out to prove his reputation to his friends. In the case of a teenage attacker, an attack would probably be motivated by his desire to be accepted by his peers or older members of his group. A recent case made me think about whether or not such an attack might be to invoke a fear of refusing a purchase. If a drug pusher cannot get you to buy his goods, why not teach a few people a lesson? It does not matter if you don't want the drug, you can always throw it away, but you must buy it.

The terrorist

A particularly dangerous facet of this attacker is that he believes that what he is doing is right and just. He may even be willing to kill himself, as well as you, supposedly to further the aims of his organization. He will not only be hardened to fighting techniques, he will most likely be well trained as well. Only under exceptional circumstances will you be able to do anything except co-operate.

Although I have referred to the attackers above as males, do not fall into the trap of thinking that boys, girls and women are not involved. In gang attacks of, say, three or four people, you may feel that the young teenager of the group can be ignored for the purposes of defence. Think again! There are far too many instances to the contrary.

Times and venues for crimes

There are undoubtedly prime times and venues for attacks, especially when such attacks are planned. The prime times are during school hours, after dark, and at wage delivery and collection times. School hours are useful to an attacker because built-up areas are relatively quiet and there is probably no more than one adult in a house. After dark is a prime time because visibility is reduced, baby-sitters are alone, people have gone to bed and so on. Wage collection times are obvious. For a planned robbery, either of the whole wage sack or of selected personnel, the results are clearly going to be more lucrative.

Planned attacks are aimed at victims where success is all but guaranteed. The housewife alone at home, the single person out shopping after visiting a bank, or the lonely walker returning home down a dark alley or a quiet pathway, are all at a higher risk level. We cannot become paranoid about this, or we would not be able to live our lives as we do. But we should seek to become aware of the danger areas and the ways of reasonably reducing the risk of being attacked. The next chapter will provide some suggestions in this area. However, what if our preventive measures don't stop an attack happening?

What to do as a victim

The diversity of attacker types (and the absence of any identification badges) means that we should treat each and every attacker alike as far as we are able. How does this work out in practice?

Probably the most important principle is to remain calm. When talking, do so in a relaxed but firm manner. If you do not do this you will open yourself up to an escalation in violence from the attacker. A circumstantial or professional mugger will feel threatened and become anxious at any delay.

He may turn to violence to speed things up. The aggressive attacker is out to show his superiority over you anyway. If you cause him to think that you would like to turn the table, he will most certainly prove his point more strongly. A terrorist is a determined attacker; no amount of shouting or resistance will make him change his mind. With the status seeker you will not always be given the opportunity to talk, but a calm mind will keep you thinking and reacting as quickly as possible. A calm mind and voice are of paramount importance.

Never offer your money. If your attacker wants it, he will demand it. Conversely, if he does not want your money, the offer may appear insulting and an escalation in violence will almost certainly ensue. Remain calm and give to the attacker anything that he asks for, in terms of your property, quickly but smoothly. If something has only sentimental value, tell him. This has the effect of showing him that you are willing to give up what he wants, and that you are calm. He may even give you the sentimental item back.

If he wants to talk then let him, but do not stall for time. Listen carefully to what he says without ridiculing him or patronizing him. Listen so as to pick up clues to his identity without making this obvious from your expressions or remarks. In fact, keep your remarks to a minimum. This approach will give you time and may enable someone to stumble across your predicament. If you live to tell the tale, any information leading to an arrest will be gladly appreciated by the police. You can only talk in this way if your attacker desires it, and you can only achieve your aims if you remain calm.

Take equal care over any attacker, regardless of height, weight, age, sex or apparent weaponry. Remember that you do not know for sure what his intentions really are. Neither do you always know whether he is armed or not. If he is armed, you do not know for sure whether or not he will use his weapon, but it is best to assume that he may do.

A difficult choice presents itself when you are faced with an attacker who wants to tie your hands and feet or cover your face. In this position you simply cannot trust the words of your attacker when he says he is not going to hurt you. If you are able to defend yourself physically, I would suggest that you do so at this point. Some burglars have tied up a family and then simply burgled their house and left. Others have picked on at least one member of the family and brutally assaulted them. If you are tied up, there is no opportunity for you to decide when enough is enough.

If co-operative methods do not cause an attack to terminate, you have only one real choice—you must defend yourself. Having said this, there may be other circumstances, such as a child in another room or obvious odds against success, that will cause you to allow an attack to continue. You may entertain the vague hope that only you will get hurt, raped or whatever. I cannot say that your choice here is wrong, any more than I can assure the person who decides to defend himself that he will be successful. Should you choose to defend yourself, I hope that chapters 9 and 10 will prove instructive.

5
Crime Prevention

Self-defence is really about keeping out of trouble rather than fighting your way out. The greater our sense of awareness, the better we will be at preventive defence. Awareness can be likened to women's intuition or a 'copper's nose'. In developing your awareness you are developing the capacity we all have within ourselves for 'knowing that things are not quite right'. Wild animals have this gift finely tuned for a very good reason—survival. As civilized beings, most of us have let our awareness faculty become lazy and ineffective. For us to survive in this world, we must rekindle the old flame.

But preventive defence is not just about awareness, it is also about common sense, training and calculated avoidance. It is common sense to take out a life assurance policy to cover family needs or lock your car when leaving it unattended. However, you and I know that not everyone does this. Training is concerned with absorbing useful information and acting on it every day of our lives. For example, do you know exactly what actions to take, and in which order to take them, if you smell gas? Would you switch on a mains voltage light in a room having a strong smell of gas? Do you know how to walk in order to make life difficult for a mugger? Can you revive a person who has stopped breathing due to electrical shock or drowning? These operations are all concerned with self-defence and preventive care for ourselves and the people around us. Calculated avoidance is concerned with such things as house security. What measures are needed to make your house and its occupants secure?

I repeat that we must not become paranoid about this. The essence of good self-defence is to know and practise preventive measures without conscious effort and strain. Since the day you were born you have been breathing without having to concentrate on it. You do it naturally. If for some reason air cannot reach your lungs, you know pretty quickly that something is not right. So it is with preventive defence. It must be practised until the effort no longer requires concentration but becomes automatic and natural. Only then will you remain calm when danger looms. You will instinctively know that all is not well and take appropriate action before it is too late. I would emphasize that there is nothing occult or supernatural about this, just as there is nothing occult or supernatural about breathing.

Making a house secure

There are two main types of thief, the opportunist and the dedicated villain. Most houses can only be protected against the former. The opportunist burglar is out for as easy a time as possible. He will quite happily skip over the well-protected house in full knowledge that easier pickings will exist.

But what is a well-protected house? On leaving a house, minimum protection consists of closed windows and mortise locks on all doors leading to the outside. Do not leave keys in the locks. A simple Yale-type lock is inadequate as one good kick will knock it clean off. If your doors are not of a suitably thick or solid design to accommodate mortise locks, change the doors. It is also worth putting a peep-hole lens into the door at eye level and attaching a good quality door chain. These items are useful for keeping out visitors that you are suspicious of. For locking up at night, use bolts at the top and bottom of doors. Unless you are very good at keeping keys near mortise locks (but not too near), you should not lock these at night. If you have to get out in a hurry, you may not be able to. Finally, some form of window lock is also advisable.

Do not fall into the trap of thinking that you have no valuables and therefore a thief will not attempt to break into your house. A thief does not know, prior to entry, that you have no expensive items. Anyway, even relatively poor people have got something of value lying around. There may be the rent money in a drawer, or a decent portable radio or television sitting somewhere. Apart from this, it may not be a thief that breaks in but one or more joy-getters who are simply out to make as big a mess of your place as possible.

If you do have some valuable equipment or jewellery, you should take more appropriate measures to safeguard them. It may be worth investing in a burglar alarm system, perhaps one that links directly into the local police station. The hinge side of external doors can be strengthened by dog bolts. These are steel pegs which slide into recesses in the door frame when the door is closed. These help to stop a door from being removed in its entirety.

The degree of protection needed depends largely on the area where you live and the aspect of the house. By far the best way of determining what would be useful while remaining 'reasonable' is to contact the crime prevention officer at the local police station. His services are free and his advice will be unbiased. You can then contact a bona fide locksmith or security equipment firm to obtain the necessary locks.

Security within a house

Whatever steps you may take, the possibility of a burglar entering your house still exists. If you are not at home, there is little you can do but trust your belongings to the alarm system (if you have one). If you arrive home and realize that something is up, do not enter the premises. Call the police and ask them to check the rooms. If you have made a mistake, the police may not be overjoyed but you will at least be safe. If a burglar is still in there, it is better that the police find him first.

But what if you are at home when the burglar calls? As always the rule of thumb is escape. You do not want to meet with him unless this is forced on you. Television plays of husbands or wives creeping downstairs, vase in hand, have a lot to answer for. You do not have any idea of how many intruders there are or whether they are armed or not. Instead make as much noise as you can, shouting perhaps for help of imaginary people. 'Fred, Dick, Harry, wake up! There's a burglar in the house!' is a good trick. If there are children in the house make your way to their rooms, opening and banging as many doors as you can on the way, but without undue delay. Once there, push a bed up against the door and get everyone to sit on it. Keep making as much noise as possible.

The new British Telecom system enables telephones to be mobile. It is worth having a telephone in your bedroom and a spare socket in the children's rooms. Take the telephone with you and contact the police once you are barricaded in. Alternatively, if you have just one telephone point in your bedroom, get the children into your room, and barricade yourselves in there and call the police. When the police arrive they will ask you to open up. If you are sure the burglar is still in the house and between you and the front door, stay where you are. The police will then make their own way in. In most cases the burglar will have vanished long ago. You can still ask the police to search the house for you, in case the intruder is hiding. A cup of tea would be a good idea at this point—for you and the police!

If you do hear a noise but are unsure about its cause, stay awake for at least fifteen minutes. This is hard to do if you were fast asleep in a warm bed. If after a short wait you are sure someone is around who shouldn't be, take the actions described above. Do try and keep an ear out for the movements of the burglar. If it is obvious to you that he is in the process of leaving, let him. Telephone the police, explaining the situation and wait for their arrival. Never go after the intruder.

Safe travelling

We are probably all aware that the law regarding seat-belts in cars has contributed to greater road safety and fewer major injuries to accident victims. In the same way, preventive defence has a few basic laws of its own and the effects are strikingly similar.

Whatever type of transport you use, be it your feet, a bicycle, a car, public transport or anything else you can think of, the basic rules are the same: stay aware of danger spots, plan your route and know where you can go for help. You may not be aware of a mugger lurking in a dark alley, but you can see the alley. Go another way. Decide before leaving how you are going to get somewhere and how and when you are going to return. Keep to lighted areas, especially if you are waiting for a lift or public transport. Never walk on the inside of a pavement. Stay on the outside third so that you can see people hiding in side-streets and behind corners. Be aware of places that will definitely be open along the route. If you do end up being chased or attacked you can escape to these places for help.

If you know you are going to drive through a notorious area, keep your doors locked. If your car breaks down, sound your horn and sit tight until a police officer arrives. Never accept offers of help from anyone else unless you know them or they are a bona fide rescue service. Do not leave your car, open a window to explain the situation or unlock a door. I would emphasize that this is appropriate action for notorious areas or any quiet but built-up area, especially at night. If a person who offers help is genuine, he will be quite happy to push you off the road, look under the bonnet, get some petrol for you, telephone a garage or do whatever else is necessary without requiring you to get out and help. You can explain through the window that you do not wish to appear rude, but experience has taught you to be very careful. Once again, a genuine helper will understand.

Car parks are prime places for muggers and rapists to operate. Try to be aware of your surroundings. If your car is parked in a dark area, have a good look around it from a safe distance. Always take a look in the back seat area before opening a front door and getting in. Just as when entering or leaving your home, make sure that you are not going to have to fumble about for the right key. Have the key ready and keep your eyes looking up and around. Countless people have been mugged outside their home or car simply because all their concentration was going into finding a key.

When travelling by foot or waiting for a lift, beware of drivers stopping to ask you for directions. This is especially important for children and young teenagers. Keep your distance from the car door or window, even if the driver appears disabled (he may not be). This is vitally important. If for any reason you would need to get close, say that you are sorry but that you cannot help and then immediately start walking in the *opposite* direction to the one in which the car is pointing. A car cannot always turn round and even when it can it takes time. Adults do not ask children for directions, they ask other adults. Similarly, adults do not ask children to help them find a pet or a lost item. If a car is obviously following you or you are suspicious about a request for directions, react in the way already indicated. Never accept lifts from people that you do not know, no matter what they say.

Always remain aware of your surroundings when travelling by foot. If you sense danger ahead, for example a group of people, cross the road and see what happens. If they cross the road in front of you, make plans to remove yourself. Where possible, enter a shop or knock on someone's door. Make it appear that this was always your planned destination. Knowing your route or being aware of your surroundings will prevent you from walking off down a blind alley. If time or place makes these options impossible, you could try walking straight up to a group and saying, 'Excuse me please,' to the group member immediately in your path. Another option, if you don't fancy your chances of success at the last move, is to turn around and walk the other way. If they start to follow you, wait until you are round a corner before taking to your heels and running. Of course, if they do start running towards you immediately you turn around, I suggest you do the same. At least you will have a head-start.

A similar approach should be adopted if you sense danger from behind. On hearing someone fall into step behind you, cross the road. If your tail follows you, cross back again. If your tail remains with you a second time, prepare to run or find help.

Using public transport

The use of public transport, especially at night, is worthy of particular note. When using buses, keep to the downstairs half and as near the driver or exit as possible. If you are about to get off and sense trouble about to follow you, wait a brief moment for the other person to disembark and then pretend to have made a mistake and go and sit down till the next stop. If you are particularly concerned, speak to the driver or conductor.

If using the underground, keep to lighted areas and mix in with a crowd whenever possible. Try not to enter empty coaches or ones that appear to have a boisterous group of people in it. If you are in the train and look like becoming a victim of some kind of attack, make plans to get off at the next stop. Do not make it obvious that you are going to leave, rather give the doors a few moments and then exit just before they close and the train moves on. Clearly you should always position yourself near an exit.

When using overground trains, once again choose your coach carefully and sit as near to an exit as possible. These trains have the advantage of toilets that can be used as escape venues, by locking yourself in, should an attack be made. You could also shout for help or pull the emergency chain if you felt the situation warranted it. Always remember that if you do not like the feel of a particular situation, trains give you the opportunity to get up and move somewhere else. This is a good test to perform.

Carrying large amounts of money

In the first instance I would simply say, 'Don't!' There are any number of ways of transferring credit or buying expensive items without having to carry around large sums of money. If for any reason at all you do have to carry a lot of cash, at least take sensible precautions. Split the money and carry it in different parts of your clothing. If you do get mugged, you can hand over your wallet or purse and hopefully only lose a part of the cash. Do not look suspicious—a mugger can often sense a person is carrying a lot of money just by the way they walk and peer at everyone. Don't grasp a pocket or keep slipping your hand in and out of it to check that the money is still there. And don't make scurrying movements that display your nervousness at carrying the money. Such movements are a beacon to the professional mugger and you will become a prime target.

If you are at a supermarket and paying by cash, try not to advertise how much money is in your wallet or purse. Get into the habit of knowing roughly how much money you will need and take this out of your purse before you reach the check-out. This will prevent prying eyes from seeing your fine array of twenty-pound notes!

The family password

One trick that a child molester may try on a child is to say something like, 'This will be our little secret, no one else must know.' Our children must be informed that this kind of secret is a bad secret, and certainly not one to be kept. There is, however, one secret that a child should keep, and that is the family password. This is a word only the family knows about. If you normally pick your child up from school or from a club but cannot make it on a particular occasion, any person who is unknown to the child and who will pick him up must be told the password. Your child will, of course, have been instructed never to go with any stranger who does not know the family password. Clearly it is sensible to change the password every so often, or you could have a password based on a rule, such as the day of the month.

Children at home

If you have children who will be alone in the house for any period of time, there are basic rules that should be observed. These rules are also of importance when you are at home with the child but are unable to answer calls of any kind due to being in the bath or whatever.

First of all, children should never answer the telephone by quoting the number. This prevents the caller from building up a rapport with the child, for example by saying how pleased he is that he had got the right number. Instead they should simply ask who is calling and who they would like to speak to. If they do not get a very obvious reply like 'Grandma', they should simply ask the caller to leave his name and number and say that Mum or Dad will return the call. To say anything more could be dangerous, as once a conversation is started the child may be tricked into divulging that he is alone. It is always a good idea if the child shouts, 'Someone's on the phone, Mum. I'll just get his name'. This will make the caller think someone else is at home, whether or not this is true.

Secondly, children should never open the door to anyone. Similar tactics to the answering of telephone calls are adequate. Overall, the rules are geared to making a caller think that someone else is at home but that they cannot come to the telephone or door at that precise moment in time. Family names and telephone numbers should never be disclosed. Do not leave items of clothing or other objects outside that bear the name of any children. Some crafty operators have fooled children by noticing these names and saying 'It's only your Uncle Albert, Peter. Be a love and open the door.'

Neighbourhood Watch schemes

These schemes have been imported more or less directly into this country from the USA. They enable members of a local community, housing estate, block of flats etc to provide some basic care for each other. Within such a framework it is possible to ensure that neighbours always go shopping in groups of at least two people, that elderly and handicapped people's needs are met, and neighbours' properties are always under limited surveillance and protection.

Watch schemes must be operated with the full knowledge and backing of the local police force and patrolling 'bobby'. If a scheme is not in operation where you live, perhaps you could get together with some other people and try and start one. If a scheme is in operation, why not join it?

There are some areas in Britain where it is never safe to go out unless there is more than one of you. Even then it is better if all the neighbours are aware of the need to co-operate with each other in times of trouble. For example, if a neighbour calls at your door to say that they are being followed, you can let them in. Your next course of action will be to call the police. In some so-called neighbourhoods people are more aggressive and alien to fellow neighbours than they are to outsiders! This is utterly foolish. In this day and age we need to be fully supportive of each other. Your Neighbourhood Watch scheme could use a password, like the family password mentioned earlier, to safeguard abuse of the help system.

Neighbours who are working for each other's benefit will be willing to help out in times of trouble. If a neighbour is being attacked in a lift, in a corridor or on the stairs, you can at least call the police and let the attackers know that you have done so. Incidentally, if you are within a block of flats or near houses and no known friends are around when faced with an attack, shout 'fire' instead of 'help' or 'police'—people are much more likely to respond this way. Also, when travelling in a lift, press all the numbers between the ground and top floors. This supplies you with multiple opportunities to escape or shout 'fire'.

Practising at home

This book contains a fair amount of theory and chapter 10 lists numerous examples of self-defence techniques. There is no way that you are going to remember all of this or, as mentioned earlier, make your self-defence an intuitive and automatic action, unless you practise. This is not the type of book that is read once and then allotted dust-space on the bookshelf.

Chapters 8 and 10 involve home practice. Chapter 8 contains numerous questions with appropriate answers plus a scoring mechanism. If, after testing yourself, your score falls below the limit set, it is time for revision.

Getting together with a partner will help you to practise the moves shown in chapter 10. There is no need to hit or throw each other. Simply practise the movements. Work at making your responses swiftly and accurately. Later on, try and counter different attacks from those shown by using a combination of, or a slight variation in, practised responses. No self-defence book can show you all the tricks. Use the few simple ones in a variety of ways to build your confidence at remaining fluid and effective.

Before practising, perform a few basic warm-up exercises like jogging on the spot, bending to touch your toes, twisting round from the hips, stretching the body upwards as far as possible and crouching down as far as possible. If you can manage it, also perform a few sit-ups and press-ups. After you have practised the techniques, exercise lightly while cooling down. Use stretching and loosening exercises to do this, such as shaking your arms, legs, hands and feet, rolling your head loosely around, lightly stretching and twisting, and circling vertically with your arms. Keep your breathing as smooth, slow and consistent as possible. Never hold your breath while exercising.

The Criminal Injuries Compensation Board (CICB)

This board is not concerned with crime prevention, but may be of use to you should you be the victim of a crime and sustain what is known as a 'criminal injury'.

The CICB is a state organization that pays compensation to

injured victims of a crime. The crime must be a 'crime of violence', though this is normally open to very wide interpretation. A prosecution or a conviction need not have occurred and even suspected crimes are included as appropriate for consideration. Claims excluded from the CICB scheme are:

(1) Cases worth less than £600.
(2) Claims for loss or damage to property.
(3) Assaults not reported promptly to the police.
(4) Claims not made within three years.
(5) Traffic offences.
(6) Where provocation existed on the part of the victim.
(7) Where claims are made by 'dubious' characters.

Although it has not always been the case, claims can be made when the injuries are due to intra-family violence, such as wife-battering. However, certain checks will be performed in such cases to ensure that the claim is not fraudulent.

To make a claim, simply write to the CICB at 10–12 Russell Square, London WC1 (tel. 01–636 4201). There is no fee for an application. A member of staff of the CICB will investigate the claim and a report will be passed on to the board. The CICB will then offer compensation as it sees fit. You may be given, and can certainly request, some guidance notes from the CICB with regard to compensation figures.

6

Helping Children

Mary and David look and act like any other normal happy children. Mary is fifteen and can still be found quietly sobbing for an hour or so at night. Sometimes the sobbing is interrupted by a short scream. The following morning she will always say that she had a nightmare.

David is an early riser except for school days. In recent months, since moving to the new neighbourhood, his love of school and learning has waned appreciably. 'Is it that the new school is not particularly academically orientated?' wonder his parents.

The truth is that Mary has been repeatedly sexually abused by her uncle since she was five. David has been picked on as easy meat by the local school bully brigade. Neither Mary nor David know how to tell their parents, or anyone else for that matter. So the agony lives on.

The preceding chapters are applicable to almost all ages, as anyone can get involved in simple crime prevention techniques. But children constitute a special group. Here I include any child up to and including adolescents. This range of ages is chosen, not because adolescents like to be treated as children in any way whatsoever, but simply because (at least in Britain) this age group consists of people who are open to similar pressures and problems.

Crimes against children

Our children face much more danger than we adults care to believe. From the very first moments of life, a child is dependent upon adult behaviour for its security and stable upbringing. It does not take very much to upset the balance, and a child starts to take notice of what is going on much sooner than we perhaps think.

Dr James Dobson, well-known writer on the Christian family, spells out most eloquently the positive strategies that can be used to build a confident adult with self-esteem, right from the early formative years. In *Hide or Seek* (Hodder and Stoughton, 1982) he says that teaching a child to be polite and kind is high on the agenda. I mention this particularly because we shall see later that these two attributes of a well-disciplined child (or adult) are beneficial in the art of personal self-defence. Dr Dobson also exposes one of our more absurd adult value systems, which makes a dipole of our attitudes towards any given child. The good-looking and intelligent we favour, and the ugly or slow-to-learn we almost discard.

It is this unjust value system that is the root cause of violence in many pre-school children. Such children inevitably become bullies or members of 'fight' gangs, and hence become a danger and a source of misery for about the same percentage of children. As if this were not enough to contend with, there are also the criminal offences that a certain element of our society wreaks upon our youngsters. These offences are enough to make animal survival warfare look like a tea-party on a country lawn. There are few depths to which some adults will not stoop when it comes to exploiting or harming children.

The existence of these dangers should hardly surprise us. Example is one of the most effective forms of teaching, therefore the society we sow is the society we reap. Each generation thus created will make life a misery for about 20–30% of the population for at least the following three generations. How stupid can we be!

Pre-school crimes

If up to infant school age a child is brought up in a loving family relationship where time with Mum or Dad is probably the most precious thing known to him, he will have got off to a roaring start in today's society. However, many children do not receive such loving care and discipline. Love as a feeling can often be a totally unknown experience. This act of rejection is the first crime against a child. President John F. Kennedy's assassin, Lee H. Oswald, serves as a stark reminder of the eventual aggression which always stems from a background of unloving parents and is accentuated if this rejection is carried on by peers throughout a lifetime.

A more common example of rejection, an almost un-intended denial of proper love and discipline, is seen in the life of Sarah. Sarah's parents were unmarried and after a couple of years of 'parenthood' they argued their way into separation. Mum now works and so Sarah is bundled off to any number of people who will look after her. Dad still often pops round to see her, but friction always exists between Mum and Dad, so his visits are becoming less common. Even when at home, Sarah has little or no time during the day devoted solely to her by Mum. Sarah is often weepy and Mum puts her to bed on the assumption that she is tired, or leaves her alone on the assumption that Sarah is simply being a little miserable at the moment.

But the truth is that the most devastating thing has happened to Sarah: she has somehow lost her parents, the two people she truly cares for the most. There was supposed to be a loyalty and a bond of trust and security between them all, but it seems to have gone.

Sarah is a fictitious character—that is, she isn't anyone in particular. Yet she exists a thousand times over in every city or area.

The crime of desertion and the lack of fulfilled responsi-bility is an acknowledged breeding ground for violent youngsters, even at pre-school age. Alternatively, the child could turn inwards and become so insecure and quiet that he is certain to be picked on to one degree or another by his peers. Life will become more and more miserable, especially as no haven is found in Mum or Dad. If you are sceptical about this, may I refer you to another of Dr Dobson's books, *Dare to Discipline* (Kingsway Publications, 1971). If a perfectly normal four-year-old is abnormally aggressive, a clear light is shining that all is probably not well at home. Even at this tender age, the example given by adults known closely to a child are readily adopted. A four-year-old knows the difference between ugly and pretty, intelligent and dim, and how the adult value system responds to such attributes. Instil violence into a child by your own actions and violent he will be. Correctly applied discipline is essential, but violence is quite another matter.

The Christian church is (or should be) an enormous family of friends and professional helpers that we can turn to if we need advice or if the going gets rough. This is especially important for single-parent families. These families need to get away from the feeling of, 'I am the only one in this mess, no one can help,' or, 'I can cope on my own, I don't need anyone to interfere.' No matter what our particular family set-up may be like, the Christian family at large exists in part to work as a complete unit for the upbringing of children in a manner that is glorifying to God.

As Christians we clearly have a duty to try and help our neighbours, though we cannot force our help onto them. Many will be the times when we see a family tearing itself apart while rejecting all forms of help. It is true that we can offer to have the children of such families for part of the day, but most of us have our own families to bring up as well. Such help can therefore be performed only on a temporary basis, and we should not feel guilty if we cannot do this for long periods or for every sad child we come across. There are times when prayer is our only option, and perhaps the only option that God intends us to use in any one case. Believe firmly in the sovereignty of God. You cannot change the world single-handed.

Self-defence for children starts straightaway. We must instil kindness, discipline, self-control and self-esteem into our children as soon as possible. No moment in time is too early. In addition to this, we should start instilling an awareness of danger into our children. This is not to frighten them, nor to make them unduly suspicious of strangers, but rather to help them recognize danger and deal with it appropriately.

There are four main types of evil that our children can be subjected to: bullying, gratuitous violence, sexual abuse and drugs. After considering each of these in turn, we will go on to see why our children often do not tell us if something is wrong, how we can help them, and how they can help themselves.

The birth of bullying

If a child with a history of neglect or violence at home has not become a bully during the pre-school years, you can be almost certain that the art will be quickly learned when at school.

But why is bullying so prevalent in our schools? Clearly one of the reasons is the home life of the child. Recent exhaustive research by Professor Dan Olweus, head of personality psychology at Bergen University in Norway, has shown that on average you can expect one in every twenty pupils to be a bully. The ratio of victimized pupils is about the same. From what has been said already, these statistics prove to be an indictment of our adult society.

There is general agreement on the reason for bullying, that of building self-esteem. The bully has not generally been accepted by adults and will therefore use his knowledge of violence to build a reputation among his peers. (Again I use the term 'he' for economy of words—girls are just as adept at bullying.) There is no concrete evidence, either from the USA, Europe or the East, to suggest that bullying is aimed at those with peculiar external features or particular academic qualities. The victims of bullies are those who can be relied on to help the bullies build their own self-image. This is why bullies tend to be bigger and stronger than their victims or roam about as a group. Girls are more likely to adopt the group method.

Gratuitous violence

Another fear that youngsters have is that of meeting up with a hostile group of youths intent on picking a fight. The motive for this hostility is similar to bullying. That is, the group members are out to build up their own images. These groups can exist within the school environment or as gangs that simply roam the area.

To build up their image, a gang will most likely antagonize their victim until the victim feels obliged to accept a fight. Cases where the victim wins in such fights are rare. Any outsider of the group is open to attack, and therefore fear of such groups is actually more widespread than the fear of being bullied.

Sexual abuse

Bullying and gratuitous violence are more often than not carried out by youngsters on youngsters. It is also perfectly common to see both male and female groups as the perpetrators of these crimes, with males and females being the respective victims. The sexual abuse of children adds another dimension to the area of crime against children. This is because adults are often involved and it is more likely to be carried out by men or boys on girls than in any other way. However, this should not lead us to assume that boys are not sexually assaulted.

Sexual abuse is not something we find particularly easy to discuss between ourselves, let alone with our children. But we are talking about crime prevention here, and sexual abuse is certainly widespread enough to make it necessary for us to teach our children how to protect themselves in this area.

Perhaps you, as an adult, have been sexually abused as a child. (If you are still keeping the pain in, my advice is,

'Don't.' Many Christians have found a great release in sharing this burden with Christian friends, their minister or a counsellor.) You will not be one of a few! Current statistics show that at least one in ten adults have been sexually abused as children. The trend has been such that the current figures for sexually abused children are at least as high as for the last two generations, and perhaps marginally higher. Furthermore, around three-quarters of all abused children are abused by someone they know and trust.

Drugs and solvent sniffing

A fairly recent danger to our children has been the increasing availability of drugs within the school environment, and the use of solvent sniffing as an alternative. Solvent sniffing has grown to include just about anything that is even remotely narcotic. Adhesives are perhaps the most widely recognized, but butane gas containers (e.g. Calor gas or Camping Gaz) and even typewriter correction fluid have been used. The Department of Health has issued a number of pamphlets and booklets that deal with both types of addiction, and a lot of government money has gone into trying to inform both children and parents about lethal effects.

As with much publicity, the message does not always get through. Your child may come under a great deal of peer pressure to 'try it out'. Unless he knows of the dangers and has a secure backing from his parents always to say no (and inform his parents of what is going on), he may feel inclined to go along with the crowd. Do not fall into the trap of thinking that 'Jimmy is such a sensible lad'. If you do not inform your child explicitly, you are running a very great risk. A recent survey in the Greater London area put the number of children who had tried solvent sniffing at one in every four. Solvent sniffing can kill more quickly than small doses of a soft drug. Addiction may not even have a chance to settle in—your child could be dead after the first round.

The danger from drugs and solvents is distinctly more subtle than either bullying or sexual abuse. The reason for this is that a child is not usually threatened in any way; it is more a matter of peer pressure. The child does not want to appear 'yellow' or a 'scaredy-cat' in front of his friends. Only an informed and loved child will be happy to say, 'My dad said that stuff will kill you and I'd rather be called yellow and live than play dumb and kill my friends or hurt my parents. Count me out!'

Why don't our children tell us?

When it comes to bullying or other forms of violence, there are a number of reasons why our children may not be willing to tell us. First of all they fear retaliation. If a bully or a member of a gang is identified as being an attacker, he or his gang friends may make life particularly uncomfortable for their informant in the future.

Secondly, there is the stigma about 'turning someone in'. For one reason or another, the child feels that 'grassing' on someone is definitely not on. Even his own friends may start to despise and ridicule him for 'telling'. This can only make matters worse, and it is therefore better to grin and bear it than take the chance of gaining even more enemies. This is perhaps the main reason why a child will not inform on his solvent-sniffing friends.

There is also the fear that Mum or Dad will overreact. A child who has been attacked may feel that his parents will also call him a 'tell-tale' or accuse him of 'not sticking up for himself'. Then again, Dad (or worse still, Mum), may decide to come to school with little Johnny, with the result that the whole school will see that he ran home to his mummy! The result of this latter action is the same as if little Johnny had spoken up to a teacher himself. The attacker is identified and so is the informant. The same fear may arise in the case of mentioning that some boys and girls are sniffing solvents or taking drugs. The child must feel that his parents will deal with the matter discreetly and sensibly.

When it comes to sexual abuse, there are additional reasons why a child may not speak up. Even though the child is the innocent party, feelings of guilt and shame will still exist. As already pointed out, most cases of sexual abuse involve someone known to the child. It could be one of the child's parents or a close family friend or relative. Imagine the emotional dilemma of being treated in such an evil way, but feeling unable to tell anyone because it would be an act of betrayal towards a trusted or loved adult. Perhaps it is a girl's father who is sexually abusing her. The girl obviously feels disgust and shame at what is happening, but the strings of child-parent love still linger and she would not want Dad to be sent away to prison or a family break-up to occur.

What parents can do to help

Perhaps the most important thing we can do is to work hard at keeping the lines of communication open between ourselves and our children. Youngsters will fail to tell their parents what is happening to them or their friends if they feel that Mum and Dad will fail to understand their predicament or will do something that will prove to be embarrassing.

If you can provide the right atmosphere for your child to share his fears, you will be in a much stronger position to offer assistance. Discuss the problem with the child and pray over the problem together. In cases of victimization or drug/solvent abuse at school, it may be that a visit to the teacher or headmaster would be in order. However, do this discreetly and at a time when the rest of the school does not receive full view. It may be expedient eventually to talk to the attacker privately, or visit his home. If you are unsure about what to do, or about how violent an attacker really is, discuss the options with other parents, the headmaster or the community policeman.

Sometimes, and particularly in the case of sexual abuse, the child will still be unable to tell anyone, even though he may desperately want to. The length of time that this agony continues will depend partly on your vigilance. I do not imply 'snooping' here, but rather a sensible and constant check on the behaviour, physical attributes and clothing of your

children. Something could easily be wrong if any combination of the following symptoms occur:

▷ Saved pocket-money becomes inexplicably reduced, or a
  child asks for money to pay for something peculiar. Often
  this is due to having to pay 'protection' money, or to buy
  drugs or solvents.

▷ Behaviour patterns are different during school days compared
  to weekends or holidays. There may be any number of
  reasons why school is causing a child some anxiety, but at
  least you can check.

▷ A child is afraid of a particular locality or person, perhaps
  crying when near someone or asked to speak to somebody.

▷ Hidden bruises or burns (e.g. from hand grips or rope).

▷ A child is quieter than normal after returning from school or a
  trip out.

▷ A longer time than normally required is being used to walk
  from one place to another. This could be due to a child being
  delayed by bullying, sexual abuse, drugs, or taking a long
  route to avoid certain areas or people.

▷ Torn clothing or damaged equipment. This can happen as
  much by design as by accident.

▷ Abrupt changes in behaviour—for example, bed-wetting.
  Some behaviour changes may be due to friction between
  Mum and Dad at home, or an addition to the family. But if
  there seems to be no obvious reason, try to find out the cause.

▷ Strange behaviour, either overactive or underactive, that
  could be caused by drugs or solvents. Also look for unusual
  nervous twitches, dilated and glazed eyes, and strange or in-
  complete speech.

▷ Abnormal interest in or knowledge of sexual matters. This
  could be due to semi-innocent promiscuity, but could be due
  to sexual abuse. Either way, things are not quite right.

▷ Inflammation or bruising around the genitals. This could be
  due to a medical problem or something more sinister.

▷ Remarks made to a child by an adult that are not in keeping with their relationship. For example, sexual innuendos or un-expected knowledge of a child's body.

With all of these signs, there are possibly very normal reasons why they exist. We should not dive in at the deep end and assume the worst. By love and understanding it is possible to enquire about these things. If the child does not respond positively, there is absolutely no point in becoming angry. This will only reassure them that telling you is not the best thing to do. If you have good reasons to be particularly concerned, keep an extra-careful watch over the following few weeks and months. Do not keep pestering the child for an explanation. Simply let it be known that you love them and that you are a little concerned for them at the moment, and then do your watching and checking discreetly.

Helping youngsters to help themselves

This is another important aspect of an adult's duty to children. As I have already mentioned, we need to start making youngsters aware of crime prevention techniques as soon as they can assimilate what is being said.

It is important to teach a child to be polite and non-aggressive. Apart from anything else, it gives the child one more way out of a physical conflict. You should explain to the child that this attitude will mark him out as a more mature person in contrast to one who quickly resorts to violence. However, the child may well have difficulty in accepting your words. He will probably regard apologizing or being polite to his attackers as weak and cowardly. You will have to spend time carefully explaining that this is not so.

Being informed and polite is applicable to many situations other than bullying or victimization. In the case of sexual abuse a child can be taught to say no in a polite and non-aggressive manner to an adult overstepping the mark. When under pressure to conform to the actions of peers, a child can simply state his case and leave. It is a great asset to a child, when under threat or pressure, to be able to say, 'My parents say I mustn't.'

Of course, there may come a time when using polite words and adopting a non-aggressive attitude will not work. A child or teenager may need to apply one or more of the physical defence procedures described in part 3 of this book. If picked on by a gang, it is surprising what a single effective technique, preferably applied to the ring-leader, will do to the morale of the rest of the group. It is always worth a youngster asking 'OK, which one of you is first?' if a single gang member is not already making that plain. The ploy may not work, but if it does it gives the child the chance of only having to cope with one of them. If he loses he is still likely to come out of it with less injuries than if the whole gang has piled in. If your child is able to restrain the first member and reinforce his wish not to fight, there is every chance that he will be left alone. All the other comments about crime prevention and self-defence tactics, as discussed in chapters 5 and 9, are also applicable to youngsters.

In the town where I live I have the honour and responsibility of running a junior aikido club for students aged between eight and sixteen. Under very strict instructions that physical conflict is the last resort, I teach them exercises, basic aikido, and non-lethal self-defence tactics. At appropriate times I will also share with them simple crime-prevention measures. As children's physical capabilities vary so widely, I leave it to your discretion to decide which of the tactics in part 3 you would want to share with your children, and when you would tell them. However, never teach them a lethal technique until both they and you are perfectly willing to face up to the possible consequences. Above all, remember that physical defence is the very last resort, and if anyone uses more force than is deemed necessary for the type of attack, they are open to prosecution.

Another way we can help is by keeping a close interest in the activities of our children. In no way am I suggesting that we should overprotect our children. The degree of protection and help we give to them will depend largely on their age and their own ability to cope. During the earlier years, i.e. up to the very early teens, we must take sensible precautions at all times. Children will pick up these habits for themselves and apply them quite naturally as they get older. Then when they do go out on their own they will be more aware of danger areas and much better equipped to deal with any eventuality.

Christian magazines such as *Buzz, Christian Family* and *Christian Woman* often mention new books and published papers that relate to the dangers facing children. The latter two magazines also contain some extremely good articles on current issues facing the Christian family in today's society. As they are published on a monthly basis, it is possible for them to give an accurate indication of current levels of crime and abuse. Libraries are another source of useful information, as is the local citizens' advice bureau. Go in at least every six months and check on any related material that may have been published recently. Above all, stay aware of the current trends and dangers. Absorb what is useful and pass on any relevant information to your children.

Finally, you might consider asking your child's school to employ the Kidscape 'Good Sense Defence' programme, if they do not already do something similar. In this programme, children are taught, at a level appropriate to their age, basic rules about keeping safe—what to do if they get lost, how to make an emergency telephone call, how to handle bullies, strangers, and sexual abuse. Information and materials are available from Kidscape, 82 Brook Street, London W1Y 1YG.

Discussing sexual abuse with your children

Although sexual abuse is a difficult subject to handle, there are a growing number of useful books and videos to help. Not all of these are particularly satisfactory, so do be careful about your choice. I first came across the following material when it was mentioned in an article by Anne Townsend on child sexual abuse. ('Forbidden Territory', *Christian Woman* magazine, February 1986):

> *Strong Kids, Safe Kids.* A video with an accompanying parents'
> handbook.
> *Preventing Child Sexual Assault* by Michele Elliott.

It's Okay to Say No! by Robin Lenett and Bob Crane. A parent/child manual for the protection of children.

I mention this material in particular because I have read or seen it all and am convinced that it is of benefit in instructing both parents and children about the dangers that exist. I have summarized below my main thoughts about all three items.

(1) The video *Strong Kids, Safe Kids* is exactly what it purports to be, a 'family guide'. It is a video for family viewing and encourages families to talk together. What a breath of fresh air! Sarah Greene introduces the video in such a sensitive way that it is clear the production team really care. Cartoon characters such as Yogi Bear, the Smurfs and the Flintstones pop up to reinforce important points. There are also songs and jingles that remind children and adults alike about the rules of safety.

At the end of the video there is about sixteen minutes of spare tape. This should be used to film your children each year. (You can hire a video camera for this purpose.) A couple of minutes' video can say so much more than a single photograph, should police need identification particulars after, say, an abduction. A fourteen-page brochure is enclosed with the video that summarizes what your children need to know and what you need to know as a concerned adult. The video was first produced in America, but this version is a British adaptation and therefore geared to the British viewer. Over two hundred British experts were consulted, including paediatricians, teachers, doctors, psychologists and so on. I would be surprised if a better video existed.

(2) Michele Elliott, educational psychologist and director of Kidscape (see above) has written a very clear and concise booklet entitled *Preventing Child Sexual Assault*. It deals with teaching children and teenagers how to prevent sexual assault, and also what to do as a parent if you find that your child or a child you know has been assaulted. At the end of the booklet there are two questionnaires testing

your newly acquired knowledge. I heartily recommend this book to anyone concerned with children and their safety.

However, there is one point in Michele Elliott's book that I do not agree with (page 22). The author says that anger focuses energy and turns thoughts into action. I believe that this is wrong, and that only clear thinking and adrenaline do this (see my comments in chapter 9). The author describes a girl called Jenny who remarked, after escaping from an attack, that her anger gave her strength she didn't know she had. This leads the author to conclude that it is beneficial to become angry at your attacker. This is erroneous. Although Jenny probably was angered by the attack and this undoubtedly caused her to react physically, her response and escape was not that of an angry person but a motivated person. I am glad Jenny started to think positively to herself, 'He has no right to do this to me.' Her physical response shows that it is possible under the flow of adrenaline to escape from an attack. It is adrenaline that gave Jenny her new-found strength. These are points worth noting. However, an emphasis on becoming angry is not a valid interpretation of Jenny's defence. As an aside, may I add that although the attack was in no way Jenny's fault, she may not have been surprised so easily if she had not been wearing her 'Walkman' while out alone.

But this does not detract from my overall impression of Michele Elliott's book. I feel that it is thorough, clear, concise and helpful. It is a worthwhile asset to any family.

(3) The manual entitled *It's Okay to Say No!* can only be described as excellent. It is broadly divided into two parts. The first is an appraisal of child sexual abuse and what parents can do about it. This is really geared to being read by parents only. The second part consists of over thirty extremely short and poignant cartoon style stories that are to be read aloud with children. Children will find it easy to relate to the context of each story, and the stories are instructive without being alarmist. The whole book

makes the reader aware that even a playgroup leader can be a molester of children, while simultaneously ensuring that respect for an adult is not lost and neither is a fear of all adults induced.

Obtaining the material mentioned

The video *Strong Kids, Safe Kids* can be purchased from Trumediastudy (Oxford), Oxford Polytechnic, Lady Spencer Churchill College, Wheatley, Oxford OX9 H1X (tel. 086 77 4850). If you simply want to view it as a family you may not wish to buy a copy, so check with your local video shop to see if they stock it.

The book *Preventing Child Sexual Assault* by Michelle Elliott is by the publishing arm of the National Council for Voluntary Organisations, in other words the Bedford Square Press. If you are in or around London you will find the NCVO at 26, Bedford Square, WC1B 3HU (tel. 01–636 4066). The book can be ordered by post from Harper and Row, Estover Road, Plymouth, Devon (tel. 0752 705251).

The parent-child manual *It's Okay to Say No!* is best obtained through your local bookshop. The revised edition was first published in Great Britain in 1986 by Thorsons Publishing Group, Wellingborough, New York. Inform your bookshop of the title, authors and publishing company, and they will be able to get you a copy. Alternatively, ask your local library to get a copy for you.

Both the books are inexpensive, being priced between £2–3 each. The video was just over £12.50 in the latter half of 1986. They are all well worth the relatively low purchase cost.

Before ending this chapter, I would also like to point you towards another recently published book, *Children at Risk* by David Porter (Kingsway Publications, 1986). This is a very general book that not only looks at drug problems and sexual abuse, but also highlights dangers to watch out for within books, TV programmes, games and home computers. The book is brilliantly researched and an absolute mine of information. Read it—and then act on it!

7
Especially for Women

Up to this point I have emphasized that your prime aim should be to stay out of trouble rather than fight your way out. This is what self-defence is really all about. We should not become paranoid about our precautions, but sensible measures should always be taken. However, there may still come a time when you find yourself in a conflict situation. After trying to escape by peaceful means, it becomes clear that you are still going to be attacked and physical methods will need to be employed (see chapters 9 and 10).

For women there are some additional facts and tricks worth knowing, and this chapter details them. However, this does not mean that men should skip over it. Perhaps when men fully realize what women have to cope with, attitudes will start to change for the better.

Self-defence for women

First and foremost you must believe, more than anything else, that you can defend yourself. Most men would take their chances if forced into a physical conflict, but for a woman this is a much more difficult decision to take. If attacked by a man in a tee-shirt you may notice that he has rather large biceps. A male victim might still decide to have a go almost instinctively (with training), but a woman would tend to have second thoughts. In this case the attacker is probably wearing the tee-shirt simply to let you know how 'big' he is. You must try and ignore such psychological tricks. After all, if he had been wearing something with long sleeves you would not have noticed and you might have decided to defend yourself. The man has not changed, only his appearance.

There are many similar ploys that an attacker will use. Imagine one of our renowned SAS or SBS men dressed in a plain pair of jeans and an open-necked, long-sleeved shirt. He would not look in the least bit aggressive. Now put him into some combat gear and stick a Balaclava on his head. What a difference! Seeing this fellow walk into a room would be enough to make anyone think twice.

Within reason you must ignore how the attacker 'looks'. He is a male with the same sensitive areas as any other male. Regardless of the size of his biceps, he will still not enjoy a blow from the heel of your shoe into the top of his foot, a strike to his groin, a good palm strike to the jaw, or grazed eyes. (You will find these techniques described in chapter 10.)

In chapter 9 the effect of adrenaline flow in your body is discussed. Once you have had some training and you can accept the fact that you can defend yourself, this adrenaline flow can be used very effectively. I emphasize this point because although the odds seem weighed against them, women more than men need to feel confident about defending themselves. For a start, there is the obvious physical difference between men and women.

Then there is the fact that women spend more time alone in houses and other buildings than most men. This means that they are inherently at greater risk. Robbers and muggers are out mainly to thieve. However, whatever the level of crime aimed at a male victim might be, a female victim will also run the risk of sexual abuse or rape. Numerous convicted rapists have admitted that they entered a house simply to commit burglary, but on finding a woman alone, they felt drawn to sexual assault.

It is the sickening crime of rape that is of special concern to us in this chapter. Rape is not just a sex crime; it is a crime of violence. It is a crime that can lead to physical hurt as well as mental anguish. Despite improvements in the way rape cases are handled by the authorities, it is still a crime that generally fails to receive sufficient justice. By this I mean that court judges are still handing out sentences that are far too lenient. For example, suppose a twelve-year-old girl who has been raped by several of her relatives over a period of years can, with the help of specially trained police counsellors, provide sufficient evidence for a conviction. If she cannot convince the court as well, because she is too upset and frightened by all the proceedings, then no corroborative evidence can be laid and the defendants will be acquitted or given suspended sentences.

This is an extreme example of British law hanging on to traditional rules to protect the rights of the defendant. I, for one, am sickened by it. At least in America, states such as Texas are changing the law to help these youngsters. No child who has given evidence under police counselling should have to face the ordeal of a court appearance. Some rapists will receive a two-year sentence, but the actual time spent in jail will most likely be less than this, while the victim's mental anguish could continue for a lifetime. Although attempts are made to 're-educate' rapists, reports in this country and America show that around 90% of rapists commit the crime again within two years of being released. All in all we have a long way to go before things start to look brighter.

I am no expert on the causes of rape or the anxieties that women face on account of it. The only thing I can do is try to convince you that you can defend yourself. I also want to dispel the trite saying, 'I'm a Christian. It won't happen to me.' Try telling that to Christian women who have been raped! Without inducing a sense of fear, I want you to be aware of special precautions and methods of defence. Nothing I say here can ever come near to making up for the harm that men cause through rape and sexual abuse. But I do hope and pray that it may save even one woman from going through the ordeal.

Profile of a rapist

Just as we looked at the profile of an attacker in chapter 4, so it will be of benefit to consider the different types of rapist. There is some disagreement in this area, which I fancy stems from a misinterpretation of terminology rather than from differing diagnoses.

Relatively few papers on rape count sexual satisfaction as a motive. This is not surprising for a number of reasons:

(1) Rape is a crime of violence.

(2) Rape victim ages range from a few months to well over eighty.

(3) Rape victims can be stunningly beautiful or very unattractive.

(4) Rapists' ages range from about eight years onwards.

(5) Rapists often report that they did not enjoy the experience, at least not on a sexual level.

However, I would not discount the possibility that sexual satisfaction can be a motive.

Although a distinction is often made between violent and non-violent rapists, I personally fail to see the difference on the basis that rape is itself a form of violence. A clearer distinction can be made if you consider rapists who are known or un-known to their victim. If the attacker is known to his victim, he is likely to employ less violence. If the attacker is unknown to his victim, the possibility of violence in the form of additional physical or sexual abuse cannot be ignored. Rape by either type of rapist can be planned or spontaneous, though consistent and violent rapists almost always plan their attacks.

Another type of rapist is the sexually excited date or the marriage partner. A problem arises here in that not only is the attacker known to his victim, but a certain degree of affection and love exists between them. The boyfriend or fiancé will not always be aware that he has gone beyond the bounds of propriety. By the time he does realize it, he may not care or it may be too late. A husband may simply desire sex with his wife and force her against her will. Initially, the husband may think that his wife is being purposely obstinate in order to excite him. This is rarely the case and only leads to further crimes being committed as time goes on. The marriage will not usually survive this thoughtless activity. In such cases counselling should be sought at the earliest opportunity.

The myths of rape

There are some very common myths about the why and when of rape. It is worth dispelling these right now.

▷ Some women and girls 'ask for it'.
   This is never true. Naïve actions may be performed but this is entirely different from willing consent.

▷ Victims rarely know their attacker.
   Wrong. On average at least 50% of rapists are known by their victims. Most of these rapists are relatives or close friends.

▷ Weapons are frequently used in rape attacks.
   Evidence does not support this. Assailants normally use fear as their weapon. Overcome your fear and you stand a good chance of escaping.

▷ Rape only occurs under given conditions.
   Wrong. Rape is committed at all times of day, in all sorts of places, against all age groups and by all age groups.

▷ Most rape victims become pregnant.
   Statistics do not support this. Very few victims become pregnant. It is more common for a victim to contract venereal disease, to which list AIDS has now been added.

▷ Women often make false rape reports.
   Only a very small proportion of women lie about rape. Similarly, children do not lie about sexual assault.

▷ Convicted and jailed rapists do not continue raping.
   Untrue. Most people who have close contact with convicted rapists know that women are at risk as soon as a rapist is released from prison. Additionally, rapists normally commit any number of assaults before being caught.

▷ Gang rapes are common.

Untrue. Groups of youths, for example, rarely go out with the intention of raping. Under the influence of drink or drugs one gang member may pick on a woman, and the others may then join in as they become sexually excited. But this is not reported as common. Very few attacks involve more than one assailant.

▷ When women say no, they usually mean yes.
What an absurd suggestion! No means exactly what it says. If a woman was joking, she would let the man know in very clear terms after he had backed off. In this instance retreat is not a sign of 'man-becomes-mouse', but a sign of respect and sensitivity that any woman would appreciate. Note that I am not talking simply of rape in this particular case—I am referring to sexual activity at any level. The argument therefore applies to boyfriends and husbands, as well as to rapists.

When reading statistics you must remember that relatively few rapes are reported to the authorities. Men's attitudes to women must change if we are to improve the status quo. Courts must apply stronger sentences and start to understand that rape is not some petty civil disturbance. Meanwhile women will have to learn to stay out of trouble as far as possible, and defend themselves successfully when all reasonable precautions fail.

Places, people and situations to avoid

Although a woman never invites rape, there are some things that women do which can only be described as naïve. 'But why shouldn't we be able to do this or that?' is the cry I often hear from girls and women alike. The reason is simple: because you stand a greater chance of being raped and sexually abused. It is no good moaning about the situation and then ignoring the warnings. You may think that there are far too many cars on the road, but you still don't cross the road without looking. The following suggestions are in addition to those given in chapter 5.

Many girls and women dress rather more daringly than they ought. Maybe this is due to misunderstanding or naïvety about male sexuality. I am not being a prude here. Prudent perhaps, but that is not quite the same thing. If I were to visit the town centre late on Saturday night, it would take me no more than five minutes to find a perfectly stunning half-naked female. This has nothing to do with fashion. Fashions change but it is always possible to remain discreet, especially when roaming the streets. I am glad to say that most Christian families ensure that their daughters and wives are pleasantly but not daringly dressed. But there are still some who take unnecessary risks, and it is those families I am addressing. It is easy for a man to think that a woman is scantily dressed for one reason and one reason only. If that is not your intention, do not dress in a way that would imply that it is.

Hitch-hiking is dangerous for females, particularly when travelling alone. This is especially true when travelling abroad. In your own country you may be able to convince the attacker that his actions are wrong and that he would not like to think of this happening to his wife, daughter or sister. You never know, you may hit home and escape the attack. But when the attacker does not speak your language, such efforts will be in vain.

To say that you should never get into a situation where you are alone with a man would be to ask the impossible. But there are some situations that should be avoided. Perhaps a boss or a colleague invites you home for coffee after a business party. Weigh up the risk. Do you know him well? Is his wife at home? Has either of you been drinking? Have you been to his house before? If not, late at night is not the best time for an introductory visit.

Perhaps you are at a celebration party in a friend's house and it has been decided that people are to 'sleep over'. In the first instance, this idea is a foolish one. Always make arrangements to get home by your own car, taxi, public transport (if you consider the route safe enough) or with another friend or relative. If you do decide to stay over, make sure that sensible sleeping arrangements have been made. Numerous cases have been reported where a girl or woman has ended up sleeping in the same room as a man. They may have known each other only since the beginning of the party or a short time before. They almost always 'crashed out' fully dressed. Rape occurred mainly because a potential risk had been entertained when it should not have been.

Baby-sitting is another danger area. The main person to watch out for is the children's father, or an elder son who arrives home earlier than expected and before the parents. I suggest that you only baby-sit for neighbours and friends that you know well and trust. Failing that, take a friend with you. Other rules such as knowing how to contact the parents, letting friends or relatives know where you are and arranging safe transport home still apply (see chapter 5). Safe transport implies use of your own, your parent's or a lift by the mother of the children. Only accept a lift by the father if you are old enough to take the decision for yourself, or if your parents have taken the decision for you, or you are with a friend for the whole of the journey and will both be getting out of the car together.

Try to get into a safety routine while alone in the house. Keep doors locked and, if you don't already have one, fit a 'thru-door' intercom and a peep-hole where appropriate (i.e. where solid wooden doors exist). If you decide to fit a door-chain, make sure it is of substantial construction. Many of these chains on the market would not be able to withstand a good shoulder barge. It is preferable to use devices that enable you to identify someone without having to open a door at all. A pushy salesman will soon give up talking to an intercom that refuses to talk further, but it is not so easy to put him off when his foot is in the doorway. If a caller is being too persistent, try calling to an imaginary person in the house or even telephone the police. Never open the door to anyone unless you know of their intentions or reasons for calling.

Similar tricks apply to answering the telephone, as we saw in chapter 6. Always imply that someone is there with you, or go 'deaf'. Obscene calls are best handled by the deaf method or a teacher's whistle near the telephone. An obscene caller wants to make you nervous—this is part of his excitement. How futile his attempts become when all he hears is 'Pardon, could you say that louder?', 'Is that you, Steve?' or, 'Oh dear, I must get this hearing-aid fixed!' The caller will soon give up. Alternatively, it will only take one loud whistle down the telephone line to convince him that perhaps it was not such a good idea after all!

If you do live alone and have a telephone, it is best to go ex-directory. Any directory entries that *are* made should be limited to initials or special titles such as 'Dr'. Never list yourself under 'Mrs' or 'Miss'.

None of these precautions, or those listed in chapter 5, will cater for every eventuality. But the risks will be significantly reduced. When baby-sitting, for example, the risk of rape will almost be limited to an attempt by someone you know. This has numerous advantages. The attacker, despite any threats that may be made, will be much less violent. He will certainly not want any injuries to show. He will be nervous about noise that may wake the children. If you are being pressed physically into a rape situation, make all the noise you can, escape from the advance and leave. Some rapists in this type of attack will try and play on your fears of making a noise and hence waking the children. Forget it! If his marriage or home life is wrecked by his actions, that is his problem. If a choice has to be made, you should protect yourself and your marriage first. Whatever your loyalty to his wife and family, an attempted rape by a friend or relative must never be endured because of it.

It is clear that you would not want to hurt a friend or relative should self-defence tactics be required. But if they are going to hurt you in terms of sexual abuse or rape, I suggest that you have little choice. It is likely that much less defence will be required to escape than if the attacker was unknown to you. As such you are not going to hurt him as much anyway. You must do whatever is necessary. A rapist is a rapist, whether he is known to you or not.

Do not plead for safety with a rapist. He wants to dominate you and you will only encourage him by doing this. Many reported cases of rape tell of the victim freezing and then pleading. Adrenaline flow will make you feel like doing this unless you know how to channel your feelings positively. You must try and think beyond whatever threats are used to make you keep quiet, especially by an unarmed rapist. If other people are close by and able to help, make all the noise you can as soon as you can. He may threaten to kill you if you scream. This is clearly a threat to make you scared and submissive. But do you know how long it takes to kill someone who is fighting back as hard as possible while screaming their heads off? It is more likely that the attacker will run away rather than try to kill you and run the risk of being caught. Think positively and think escape.

Repelling a rape attack

After all reasonable precautions have been taken, the possibility of facing a rape attack remains. Should this happen to you, I hope that the material in chapters 9 and 10 will prove helpful. However, there are other rules and tricks that can be employed to prevent an attack being successful.

In deciding to use force, the quicker you react the better. Clearly the chances of you being harmed are much reduced the sooner you escape. You can escape more easily and quickly if the rapist is not in a position to commit the crime. Try to react before you end up on your back—that is, while he is dragging or pushing you to a particular spot. Adrenaline flow will start to make you feel very insecure and unable to fight, unless you react swiftly or something happens to snap you out of your defeatist frame of mind. Make your move, if at all possible, within twenty to thirty seconds of an attack becoming obvious to you. Though it may not seem like it, this is quite a long time within which to make a decision.

In making your move, you must go for broke. You must do whatever is reasonable in order to escape (see chapter 9). A rapist is there to dominate you. A rapist wielding a knife is probably doing so because he feels unable to control the situation without it. Either way, once you start to make it plain that you are not going to submit, you are breaking whatever pathetic sense of dominance he has. You must escape! If your attempt fails, you run the risk of being hurt more than your attacker originally intended. Your defence, if swift and decisive enough, will surprise your attacker as well as create an opening for you. Use this surprise element to its maximum effect. Above all, believe in yourself.

Sometimes a useful aid to escaping from a potentially dangerous situation is that of the hand-held rape alarm. These can be purchased from all manner of places including super-markets, hardware stores, chemists and locksmiths. They emit an extremely loud high-pitched noise, with the intention of frightening an attacker away and drawing notice to your plight all in one go. However, never rely on them to do their intended job without first obeying all the precautionary rules with regard to self-defence. Also ensure that you can remain aware of all movements around you while this intense noise exists. These alarms are of use in Neighbourhood Watch schemes where neighbours are aware of the sound and the reasons under which they would be used (i.e. not necessarily rape).

Another way of repelling a rape attack is to try and con-vince the attacker that you are suffering from some form of contagious illness. This may shock you, but a good example would be to say that you are under treatment for VD. He may not believe you, but if he is the slightest bit suspicious he will probably leave you alone. What you are effectively doing is removing his desire to commit the crime. You could try 'go-ing crazy'. I do not mean that you should attack him wildly, but that you should take on the response of a woman already raped a few months earlier. Exclaim your horror amidst streams of tears, letting him know what has (supposedly) happened. Pretend to faint. You may touch the human side of his nature and he may leave. If he continues his attack, the last thing he will be expecting is a palm strike to the jaw or a blow to the groin or solar plexus!

The desire to commit the crime can also be removed by vomiting. This is easily achieved by sticking two fingers down your throat. The chances of the trick working are about the same as any other. Some attackers will become angry at the attempt; others will not wish to stay around.

Stories exist of women convincing rapists to come back the next day (on account of the fact that their parents are coming shortly or whatever), or of persuading their attacker to let them go home, wash, slip into something appealing and then meet again. Of course when the next meeting does occur it is the police that meet him, not the proposed victim. As these stories are true, I can only say that the trick does sometimes work. I am doubtful, however, about the effectiveness of the trick compared with the others mentioned.

Rape trauma syndrome

What if you have been unsuccessful in your attempts to repel the attack, and rape has occurred? Rape trauma syndrome is the term that is used to describe the shock and mental anguish that a rape victim invariably goes through. Outward signs vary between hysterical behaviour and pure numbness. Delayed mental and physical breakdown often occurs. Victims feel guilt and shame at the degradation they have had to endure. Sleeplessness, nightmares and an inability to relate physically to men (including boyfriends and husbands), no matter how sensitive and caring they may be, are some of the problems that arise.

Experience supports the view that the sooner a woman can start to talk about her ordeal, the quicker will be her recovery. Coming to terms with the situation takes time, effort and a lot of patience. The process of restoration is best started as soon after the attack as possible. Some women will be able to talk quite soon, while others will hold on to their grief for years. Occasionally a woman will never be able to do this and a whole life is as good as ruined.

Getting help after an attack

You may turn to any number of people for help and counselling. Immediately after an attack you will most probably turn to a friend. A friend can be both comforter and witness to your emotional state. This will become important as we shall see. For counselling and other information you could turn to your pastor or vicar or some other church worker. Alternatively you could contact CARE Trust, 21a Down Street, London W1Y 7DN (tel. 01 499 5949) who will try to put you in touch with a Christian counsellor near you.

Nationally there are also the Rape Crisis Centres run by trained women for women. They provide counselling help, usually over the telephone, for girls and women who have been raped or sexually abused. There are five main centres and many more smaller groups dotted around the country. The telephone numbers for the major centres are:

London	—	01-837 1600
Exeter	—	0392-30871
Birmingham	—	021-233 2122
Manchester	—	061-228 3602
Edinburgh	—	031-556 9437

For your local centre you should look in the local directory, call directory enquiries or contact one of the main centres listed above. Counsellors will, if necessary, be willing to escort women to police stations, hospitals and so on. Calls are treated in the strictest confidence.

It does not matter where you go for help, as long as you go. This is easy for me to say in that I am not a woman and I have not been raped. I say it only because I believe that it will be to your ultimate benefit. You may prefer a Christian counsellor or friend, and this is understandable, but the Rape Crisis Centres have very experienced staff. Remember that getting help is not the same as reporting the crime or pressing charges should the rapist be caught. Getting help is about rebuilding your shattered world. Reporting a crime is the legal entrance to seeking some form of justice through the courts.

Reporting a rape attack

Once again this is easy for me to say, but I would hope that every Christian woman raped would report the fact. This takes a lot of courage and the police medical examination and statement-taking processes are far from minor.

If you are going to report the attack, you must do it as soon as possible. Failure to do so will result in loss of evidence. Do not change your clothes, or go to the toilet, or wash. If you must change your clothes, take the clothes you were wearing to the police station with you. For your own comfort take a close friend or relative with you. They will be allowed to stay beside you during the medical examination and the taking of your statement. Be prepared for a long day.

The police medical examination is performed simply to collect evidence. Traces of hair, sperm, clothing and saliva will be tested in all parts of your body where rape or abuse was conducted. Many women have thought of this as the second rape. It is one of the reasons why it takes a lot of courage to report the incident in the first place. You can request that a female police doctor perform the examination, but in this case don't be surprised if you have a long wait. Alternatively you can ask that the examination be performed by your own GP or a female GP in the same practice. Your emotional state will be recorded as well as your physical state. If you went to a friend immediately after the attack, she can act as a witness to your initial appearance.

Then there is the statement. You can insist that a woman police officer takes this and the police will comply whenever possible. However, there is no legal obligation for them to do so, unless the victim is under 16, when a woman police officer must be used. The statement is an important legal document. If you become tired or upset by the pressure, take a break or come back the next day. Read the statement carefully before signing it. If you disagree with any of the wording used by the officer, say so and get it changed. Never, never sign this document unless you are satisfied that all is correct.

Physical injuries

Remember that the police medical examination is for evidence only. If you have suffered physical injuries you will still have to visit a hospital. Venereal disease can be contracted through rape and a priority appointment can be made at a clinic for you. There will be no evidence of such disease for around seventy-two hours after the attack, so make your visit between four and seven days later. Venereal disease can be treated and stopped if reported early. You should also obtain the current information on testing for the AIDS virus.

Rape also brings the fear of pregnancy. If you were not using a contraceptive such as the pill or an IUD, the risk of pregnancy is of course higher, but it is still not very great. You can almost ensure that pregnancy is not allowed to develop by taking what is known as the 'morning-after pill'. This consists of a dose of oestrogen and progestogen equivalent to about six normal pills, and prevents the fertilized ovum from implanting itself in the womb. The police or a counsellor may mention this option to you so it is as well to know about it. You will need to decide how you feel about this sort of action, whether you regard it as a form of last-minute contraception, or more akin to a very early abortion. If you do consider it as a viable option, then speed is of the essence, because the pill will only work if taken within seventy-two hours. Even within this period of time, you stand a greater risk of full pregnancy the longer you wait. Nausea and sickness are common but short-lived effects. The pill is only about 98% effective and about 3% of babies born after the dose has failed suffer from some congenital abnormality. As such, termination will be offered to any woman who becomes pregnant after taking the pill, and again, you will have to decide whether such an action is morally justified in such circumstances. A full discussion of the ethical issues—what constitutes abortion, and is it ever right even after rape?—is beyond the scope of this book, but you will find that Christians don't always agree on these questions.

Other injuries sustained will depend purely on the attack. Perhaps the real trauma is that after a rape attack, all you will feel like doing is hiding and protecting your private parts. But examinations and the healing of injuries are necessarily aimed at such parts of the body. There is no way around this except to follow Paul's advice: 'By prayer and supplication with thanksgiving let your requests be made known to God. And the peace of God, which passes all understanding, will keep your hearts and minds in Christ Jesus' (Philippians 4:6–7).

The court case

If the attacker is found, the police will draw up a case against him. You will be informed of the arrest and, unless you say otherwise, it will be assumed that you wish to press charges. You can decide not to continue but the police will not be too happy. After all, they have spent valuable time and resources looking for this man. You will have to sign a withdrawal form if you do decide to go no further.

You may also be asked to identify the man in an identity parade at the police station. This will be a strain for you, but it will help the police to make the prosecution more sound. Two-way mirrors can now be used so that you can view the parade without being seen yourself.

Within a couple of months of the arrest taking place, a magistrates' court will decide if there is enough prosecution evidence to warrant a full crown court trial. This is the 'committal proceedings' stage, for a rape charge can only be heard at crown court level. You may not have to attend the magistrates' court because the Criminal Justice Act of 1967 introduced a 'committal on the documents' procedure. This means the magistrates can accept prosecution evidence in writing, i.e. previous statements and so on. However, this cannot be guaranteed, as the defendant may insist on your presence even at this stage.

The crown court trial by jury could happen at any time after the magistrates' decision. Usually you will have to wait for anything up to twelve months. The case will rely heavily on your original statement and you should read and study this before going to court. Make sure it is clear in your mind and that you are convinced about what happened. (Of course, if the rapist pleads guilty, which is rare under British law, you may not have to attend the trial at all.) You will be questioned first by the prosecuting council (who is on your side and trying to achieve a conviction). Then the defence will be given the chance to cross-examine you. This is a most trying experience. You will normally have to tell everything in the smallest detail, and that in front of some fifty or more people. Your attacker will also be present. The defence will more than likely try to discredit your story. He is not in the least bit interested that you are a Christian and hence 'above' lying. After you, other witnesses will be called, and some of these may be able to vouch for your lifestyle. The police may encourage you to leave the court room during this period because it is felt that if the jury sees a woman calmly listening to evidence, they might consider that the attack was not that bad. Do not leave permanently, however, as you may be called back for further questioning.

After all the interrogation has been performed, the prosecution and defence barristers will make closing speeches. The judge will sum up the case and the jury will retire to reach a decision. If the defendant (your attacker) is found guilty, he can face anything up to life imprisonment. Sadly, as we have seen, the actual sentences pronounced are much less severe. Under British law, if the defendant is acquitted he will go free and the prosecution cannot appeal. If the defendant is convicted, all manner of things could happen to try and make the sentence as lenient as possible. The defence can also appeal against the sentence itself, or a point of law, or the jury's decision. The jury can only find the man guilty or not guilty, they have no control over the sentencing. If at least ten of the jury of twelve cannot come to a conclusion, a new trial will be ordered.

In conclusion

No one can deny that rape is a most brutal form of violence. The trauma that women have to face is not yet matched by the lenient sentences that are often awarded. This, plus the necessary legal and medical examinations, deter many women from actually reporting the crime. They feel that it is better to suffer one rape than have to go through the examinations and court appearances as well, knowing all along that the sentence may not be worth the effort even if the case is proved. Only the victim in question can make that decision. However, there is no doubt that a rapist off the streets, for any length of time, is better than a rapist left to roam.

The improvements that police have made in the handling of rape victims—and indeed continue to make—must be for the good. More women will be willing to come forward if they know that they will be treated sympathetically. Remember as well that despite the ordeal of a court appearance with reporters present, your name and address are legally protected and must not be published.

If you take reasonable precautions you will lessen the possibility of rape being threatened. If you can fight your way out of an attack and escape, you will have succeeded in removing much grief that would inevitably ensue. Report even *attempted* rapes to the police. If a man is working the area, the police will soon get to know about it and possibly apprehend him before any further damage is done. If rape is committed you will have to decide whether to report it or not, unless the rape is part of a wider crime in which case the police will be involved anyway. If you do report it, remember that you are entitled to compensation from the CICB as detailed in chapter 5. In addition, the probationary service operates a Victim Support Scheme, which provides an explanation of the court procedures in which you will be involved, together with further counselling as necessary.

Whether you decide to report the incident or not, do get experienced help with the trauma that you will experience to one degree or another.

8

Know the Game

Think of a subject that you have stopped studying or following for at least a year. How much of it can you remember? I doubt very much if you can recall all of what you used to know. To remain well versed or good at something, we must all continue to practise and stay abreast of things. Hence the following short tests.

In each of these tests there is a varied number of questions. You must award yourself two marks if your answer is correct, one mark if only partly correct and zero if you answer incorrectly. This is the marking scheme for each question. At the end of each test there will be a revision score level. If you ever score less than this test level, you should revise appropriate chapters and do any necessary background reading or research.

In most cases the model answers provided at the end of this chapter will be enough to correct your mistakes. However, individual chapters of this book contain more general information than these questions ask for. Falling below the revision level probably indicates that rereading would also be beneficial.

No questions are asked on the techniques shown in Part 3. This has been done deliberately so as to restrain you from feeling that there is only one correct response to a physical attack. I would much rather you practised the physical techniques with a friend and 'felt' their application rather than answer theoretical questions about the techniques.

Test 1

1. A mugger wants to succeed in two main things. What are these?
2. A mugger grabs at your wallet or handbag. What do you do?
3. 'Young or female muggers are not as dangerous as adult muggers.' Is this true or false for both types mentioned?
4. If a mugger confronts you, remain calm and simply offer him your money. Are these two actions sensible?
5. There are two ways to avoid being surprised by a mugger in a lane or hiding in a doorway or round a corner. How?
6. What should you do, and conversely not do, when approaching a door to unlock it?
7. In addition to the answers to question 6, what extra precautions can you take when returning to your car, especially at night?
8. Would you automatically allow an attacker to cover your face with something, or tie your hands and feet?
9. What are the two danger signs that signify that you are being followed?
10. Preventive self-defence is about four things. What are these hallmarks?

[Test level: 17]

Test 2

1. What are the two types of house burglar?
2. 'A burglar will not bother to enter a house with no valuables in it.' Discuss this in a few sentences.
3. What are the minimum operations to perform when leaving a house for any length of time?

4. On returning home you suspect that someone has been inside. 'You should find out what is missing and then phone the police if necessary.' True or false? Why?

5. If you think you can hear a burglar in the house at night, how long should you stay awake?

6. On knowing a burglar is in the house at night, what steps would you take if there are children?

7. You are travelling by car in a quiet area (built–up or in the country), and you break down. As a woman, what actions should you take if the situation appears risky?

8. Your daughter comes home and tells you that a man stopped his car to ask her for directions. The man was disabled and so she leaned on the open window to explain the route on his map. She made two mistakes; what were they?

9. You suspect that you are being followed by a vehicle. What should you do?

10. If you sense danger ahead while out walking, what two things can you do? If you feel the need to run, when should you start running?

11. When using public transport at night, what are the main golden rules?

12. When carrying large amounts of money, what are the main golden rules?

13. What is the family password system, and what is its main usage?

14. There is one thing you should do before exercising and one more thing on finishing. What are these?

15. When answering the telephone, what should a child never do?

16. Why should you never leave an object outside the house or let your child wear clothing that displays the child's name?

17. There is one thing a child can always say when someone calls at the door or telephones, whether or not the child is alone. Suggest a phrase.

18. If a stranger asks your child to go with him for any reason at all, in any place, what must your child do?

19. If you are alone in a lift, what main precaution should you take?
20. If attacked near houses or in a block of flats, what should you shout in order to arouse help?

[Test level: 35]

Test 3

1. By way of example there are at least five qualities we can instil into our children to help them feel secure. What are these qualities?
2. There are four main areas of danger for our children when outside the home. Name these categories.
3. 'Most children are sexually abused by strangers.' True or false?
4. 'Solvent sniffing is not very widespread, and those who do try it are in less danger than when trying mainstream drugs.' True or false?
5. 'Solvents used for sniffing are limited to adhesives.' True or false?
6. Why is solvent sniffing a more subtle danger to children, compared to, say, bullying or sexual abuse?
7. Why do child molesters often get away with the crime for so long?
8. What four things can we do to protect our children from child sexual abuse?
9. What is the main thing adults can do to help protect their child from danger, while not smothering them?
10. There are at least three sources of information for keeping up to date in family defence. List these sources.

[Test level: 17]

Test 4

1. Explain the two different responses that can result from adrenaline flow in an attack situation.

2. In an attack on a woman, what trick can a man use to put his victim off resisting him?

3. What areas of the body should you aim for, and with what natural weapons, if you need to escape from an attacker?

4. 'Rape is simply a sex crime.' True or false?

5. 'A woman must have provoked a rape attack in one way or another.' Discuss.

6. 'A rape attack will only occur under given circumstances.' True or false? Why?

7. 'Jail sentences are a good deterrent for rapists, and few will commit the crime again after leaving jail.' True or false?

8. When confronted with an attack by a person known to you, what should you do when other adults or children are near, even if he threatens to harm you?

9. To reduce the possibility of a rape attack, what precautions can be adopted?

10. If alone at home (especially at night) what precautions can be taken to keep intruders out?

[Test level: 17]

Answers to the tests

The answers given here are neither exclusive nor conclusive. Further, they are by necessity relatively brief. However, the answers will be able to point you in the right direction. Note once again that these tests are not exhaustive of the material covered in this book. They are just 'samplers' to keep you thinking about defence procedures.

Test 1

1. A mugger wants your valuables and he wants to get away without being caught. Enable him to achieve this and you will usually remain unharmed.

2. As in question 1, let him have what he wants so that his

crime may succeed and you may escape injury. Without letting your attacker realize it, try to see what he is wearing from the waist down and also what he looks like. Inform the local police of the attack.

3. False in both cases. The young or female attacker is every bit as deadly as the 24-stone heavy.

4. Yes, it is sensible to remain calm, and training will help you to do this (though you will still feel fear). However, never offer your money. If a mugger wants your money, he will ask for it.

5. First of all you can avoid going down a lane, particularly if it is dark. Secondly, you should walk on the outside third of a pavement or the middle of a narrow alley or lane.

6. Always have the appropriate key out ready in good time. It is a mistake to approach a door and then put all your concentration into finding the key. Stay alert and looking up and around.

7. First of all a car should be left in a well-lit area at night. On approaching the car, look around it before getting too close. Always look in the back seat before getting in.

8. No, not automatically. The decision is not always yours to make, but where possible you should talk or fight your way out of this situation. Tell your attacker you have brittle bones or can bleed internally easily. Tell him he can take what he wants but that you remain as you are. Always look to escape from this type of attack as you cannot trust an attacker who wishes to limit your sight or limb movement.

9. Your tail will very likely fall into step with you and follow you if you cross the road. He may also stop when you do and then follow you when you continue.

10. Common sense, training, prevention measures (e.g. locks) and awareness of surroundings.

Test 2

1. There is the opportunist who will always go for the easy

pickings, and the professional (dedicated) villain whose burglaries are usually well planned. The latter knows what he is after.

2. Not true. How does he know that there are no valuables until he is inside? Once inside he can cause a lot of damage anyway, and perhaps find a woman alone and commit rape.

3. Shut and lock all windows (including the bathroom window) and doors. Do not leave keys in locks. If you have a burglar alarm, set it.

4. False. Telephone the police by all means, but do not enter the house yourself. The burglar may still be inside.

5. At least fifteen minutes.

6. Make as much noise as possible. Switch lights on. Shout for help from imaginary members of the family (male names). Bang doors. Get to the children's bedroom and barricade yourself in. Keep making a lot of noise. If you have a telephone point in the children's bedroom, take a telephone with you and call the police. Try and listen for the burglar leaving. Always let him leave and never investigate while you think he is still around.

7. Lock all doors, close all windows, sound your horn and wait for help. If you have warning lights on your car, use them as well.

8. She assumed that adults ask children for directions (rare), and she went too close to the car. She should have said, 'No, sorry,' and kept on walking or doubled back the other way.

9. Turn around and walk the other way. Walk down a one-way street the wrong way, enter an open building, or head for a nearby pedestrian precinct.

10. Walk into a shop or garage, call at a house or make some pausing gesture (e.g. checking the time) and turn around and walk the other way. If wide enough, you could cross the road to be well out of their path. If at all possible do not run until you are round a corner. In this way they cannot see you take to your heels.

11. Do not enter transport that contains suspicious or rowdy

people. Stay downstairs in buses. Sit or stand near an exit or the driver. Where possible face all other passengers.

12. Try not to look like a prime target by holding a pocket tightly or continually checking if the money is there. Split the money about your person. But avoid carrying large amounts of cash unless absolutely necessary.

13. It is a secret word that only the family knows about. It can be used to enable a child to accept a lift from a person unknown to him (a thing he should never normally do). Useful in emergencies.

14. Warm up to start with, and cool down while exercising lightly when finishing.

15. A child should never mention the telephone number, the names of any family members, or the fact that he is alone.

16. A would-be attacker/molester would use the name to try and fool the child into thinking that the person was in fact bona fide.

17. 'Mum (or Dad) can't come to the phone just now. I'll go and tell them you called.'

18. Say no, walk away, and tell you what happened.

19. Press the numbers for all floors. This supplies you with a maximum number of opportunities to escape or shout 'Fire!' It also distracts your attacker and he is more likely to be spotted committing the crime.

20. It is best to shout something like 'Fire!' People may not always help if they feel they may get mugged as well.

Test 3

1. A stable child will understand kindness (love), discipline, self-control, self-esteem and be aware of danger areas.

2. Bullying, violence for its own sake, sexual abuse, and drugs.

3. False. Only about 20–25% of child molesters are unknown to the child.

4. False on both counts.

5. False. Even typewriter correction fluid has been known to be used. Butane gas canisters are another source.

6. Because it is usually peer pressure that is the driving force. This is not always easy to recognize or to resist. A child must be confident of his parents' leading and control if he is to stand a chance of survival against unhelpful or dangerous peer pressure.

7. The child abuser may be a trusted member of the community and almost above suspicion. He or she will most likely be known to the child and the child will not be able to tell anyone. The child, if first attacked at an early age, will perhaps not realize that the act is abnormal.

8. Believe them when they tell you. Teach them when to say no to an adult. Explain to them what a 'bad' touch is, and what a 'bad' secret is.

9. Overall it is to keep the lines of communication open. This takes time and devotion to the family as a whole. With the pressures on a modern family unit this is not easy to achieve, but is nevertheless essential.

10. Magazines (Christian or otherwise), libraries and the local citizens' advice bureau.

Test 4

1. Without training you are likely to become frozen, unable to respond or even believe that the attack is in fact happening. With training you can acknowledge that your fear is a sign of your body working and that you could respond with strength and energy if need be.

2. He can make himself look rough by not shaving and wearing clothes that show his muscles off as much as possible.

3. Natural weapons to use are your foot, knee, fist, outside edge of hand, palm of hand, fingertips and nails. Areas to aim for are the knees, groin, solar plexus, kidneys, throat, chin, nose and eyes.

4. False. It is a crime of violence.

5. False, because of question 4. A rapist needs no other motive or stimulus. A woman can be naïve, but that is not the same thing.

6. False, mainly on the basis of statistics. Rape occurs at all times of the day in all sorts of places.
7. False on both counts. Most rapists will commit the crime after leaving prison, even when they have received some form of counselling while inside.
8. Shout your head off, fight and plan to escape. This type of attacker is unlikely to want to hurt you and is calling your bluff. It takes a long time for an untrained person to kill another person, particularly when the victim is not being exactly passive about it.
9. Dress reasonably and discreetly. Do not hitch-hike. Only go out at night with someone else, and always get safe transport home. Avoid known danger areas.
10. Keep windows shut and locked in rooms other than where you are, and all doors locked. Never let a telephone caller know that you are alone. Never open an exterior door without first looking and checking, and use a door chain if necessary when talking to the caller. Close curtains at nightfall.

PART 3

Self-Defence Techniques

9
Using Physical Self-Defence

On the assumption that you have read at least the preface or some of the preceding chapters, you should by now be aware that resorting to physical self-defence methods is the very last thing you should do in any conflict. If there is any other way out of the situation, take that way. There may come a time, however, when you will have to fight back. Notice that I use the term 'fight'. At the end of the day, self-defence is not fun. Physical techniques are brought into play because you feel that if you don't do something, your life or the life of another person will be in danger. There can be no half-measures here. Although you will be acting in defence, your actions will be of controlled aggression. Make no mistake about this.

The feeling of fear

When faced with a life-threatening situation there is no doubt that you will feel fear. Do not be surprised at this or afraid of the feeling itself. It will not matter whether you are fight-hardened, experienced in self-defence tactics, or a complete novice in the art of fighting; you will still get the feeling.

The reason for this is quite natural. At the upper end of each of your kidneys there are two pyramidal adrenal glands. The inner core of each gland, called the medulla, secretes the hormone adrenaline under the direct control of your nervous system. Adrenaline will increase your heart rate, raise your blood pressure, and increase the glucose level in your blood. Its end purpose is precisely to prepare you for 'fight or flight'. When frightened your sticky hands, pounding heart, shaking limbs, and jelly-like legs are simply a sign that your adrenal glands are functioning.

This means that, should you decide to take action, there is enough 'fuel' being pumped around your body to cope with the high level of activity that is likely to occur. However, problems arise on two counts. First, you may be so nervous that the amount of adrenaline produced makes you 'freeze'. You feel that you simply cannot move and must therefore submit to whatever is in the attacker's mind. This feeling is only exacerbated by the second problem that can occur. Under stress you may feel that all you want to do is hide. You may experience thoughts like, 'This is unreal,' 'I am imagining this,' or, 'This cannot be happening to me.' Your final choice between freezing, fleeing or fighting will, I believe, depend on training.

Trained fear

Why do I believe that training will make a difference? Well, first let me say why I believe that lack of training will often lead to a person freezing solid. When reading reports of rape, I often see that the woman says, 'I always thought I would scream, kick and shout my head off. But I didn't, I just froze and pleaded with him not to hurt me.' This is the effect of an untrained person's adrenaline flow. They always thought they would fight, but because they had little or no training in how, they simply didn't. I am not being condemnatory here, though I do wish people would not keep saying, 'It will never happen to me,' and do nothing in terms of precautionary measures. I am simply stating an observation.

Another observation, one that leads me to believe that training does help, is simply the existence of men and women in our civil and armed forces. We would not expect a policeman to freeze as soon as he came across a dangerous situation. Neither would we expect a soldier to be incapable of fighting when called on to do so. Yet these men and women have only one major difference in their background from anyone else— they are trained. I have talked to a number of policemen and armed forces personnel and all of them have said they feel nervous and fearful at times of stress. But it does not stop them from acting positively.

Another important aspect of training is the creation of awareness. Both the police and the armed forces are trained first and foremost to stay out of trouble. If something is going wrong somewhere, the first option is always to try and remove yourself from the danger area. The points raised in chapter 5 should never be taken lightly. It is possible that sensible precautions and an acute sense of awareness will stop you from ever having to resort to force. Professional martial artists spend their entire life perfecting their deadly art, always in the sincere hope that they will never be required to use their skills in a moment of true conflict. They hope that their training in awareness will protect them from ever getting into such a situation. This is the only way to treat your training, however intense or minimal it may be.

Keeping a clear mind

Throughout an attack it is imperative that you stay as calm as possible and keep your mind working. Some of the reasons for this have already been discussed in chapter 5. Regardless of any training or any degree of awareness on your part, you may still find yourself in the middle of a conflict.

A clear and calm mind will stop you foul-mouthing your attacker or making the mistake of telling him he cannot have the money or goods he has asked for. Both these actions are about the worst you could take. If an attack was not intended to be violent initially, it may turn out that way if you do not co-operate. If an attack is going to turn violent, or it was a simple attack of violence in the first place, you may still be able to deter your assailant from carrying through his attack.

I have already mentioned some ideas related to avoiding rape, in chapter 7. There are also stories of victims telling their attackers that they are haemophiliacs (i.e. they bleed easily and profusely, both externally and into their joints) or they have brittle bones or a serious heart disorder. Their plea is along the following lines: 'I know you can beat me up, but I suffer from this medical condition. If you attack me you will most probably maim me for life or kill me. I cannot stop you from doing what you want, but I want you to realize the consequences.' This has been known to make an attacker who is out merely to show his dominance over his victim back away, giving only a verbal warning to the victim not to do anything to try and get his attacker caught. Of course, if an attacker is out to kill you or his mentality is such that he wants to hurt you badly, the trick will fail and you will have to resort to physical defence. Even now you will have the advantage as the attacker will not be expecting you to fight.

Another story is told of a boy who was robbed of his pocket-money by a gang, and then informed that he was going to be beaten up anyway. Realizing that he was no match for them, he suggested, 'You guys know you can beat me up, but if you let me go I'll bring you more money tomorrow.' They let him go and he promptly went home and told his dad what had happened. The next day his father approached the gang and informed them that they had stolen once from his son and he would ignore that, but if they tried it again there would be trouble. Within a couple of days a few members of the gang again approached the boy. This time it was not to 'deal' with him but to return his original money! Once again, there is no guarantee that this or any similar approach will work in any one case, but it is better to try and avoid a physical encounter if at all possible.

Three steps to the plunge

There will be three stages to your eventual use of force to protect yourself or someone else. You must first clearly decide whether or not force is to be used. If it is, you will need to consider what is available to help you. Finally, you will need to remember that the sole purpose of your physical activity is to enable you to escape—nothing more, nothing less.

The most important rule is never to use force to protect property, only people. Remember our comedian in chapter 2, who was actually trying to decide whether he wanted to hand over his money or be killed for it. Clearly the humour is in the utter folly of the situation. No matter what the commercial value of your loss may be, it will not be as valuable as your life.

It is a sad observation that although you may agree with me now, you may not agree on the spur of the moment when a crime is being committed. Countless men have been seriously injured because they reacted impulsively during an attack, usually trying to protect very small amounts of money. Many women have been assaulted during what could have been a simple handbag snatch operation because they wouldn't let go of their bag. This is another reason why training is important. We need to train ourselves not to hold on to material goods. This is especially pertinent to Christians, as I have said before. If you do need to have valuable equipment or goods for any reason at all, you should get it insured. Insurance is not un-scriptural and should be carefully considered. It should have the effect of actually making us less anxious to hang on to material things.

Taking into consideration all that has been said so far, we need to have some clear guidelines as to when we should use force. You must make your own decisions over this, though I would mention some basic pointers to help you. An attacker who demands goods, whether armed or not, should be granted his every wish. Most attackers will be happy with this and leave you alone after taking what they want. However, if your assailant continues his attack, making definite noises and moves to make you believe that he is going to beat, disable or kill you, you have no alternative but to make the decision to use force or be abused. As I have already mentioned in chapter 7, if you are a woman and an attempted rape is being forced on you, you will need to decide whether to put up with the mental and physical anguish of the attack, or to treat the attack as any other and fight to escape.

In all cases, remember that an attacker who says he is only after your money or your body may not be telling the truth. I would suggest that an attacker who says that he will not hurt you, but wants to bind your hands or legs or cover your eyes with something, is probably lying. Of course, he may just be restraining you for some other reason, perhaps to prevent you from getting help quickly or recognizing him if he decides to remove a mask. If your hands or feet are tied, you are in no fit state to offer resistance if an attack turns violent. If your eyes are covered, you will not be able to watch his movements.

Once you have taken the decision to use force, you must be prepared to use any and every asset available to you. Some of the things I say here may offend your Christian conscience. If so, I apologize in advance. Physical combat is not a game, and defence tactics will not work if done in a half-hearted way. You are only resorting to combat as a last attempt to protect yourself, so do it effectively. Remember that you can always get medical help for an attacker if you have hurt him badly. The attacker will not do likewise for you. Remember that all you are trying to do is escape with as few injuries as possible, both to yourself and your attacker. In the vast majority of cases you will do much less harm to your attacker than he would do to you. Any injuries sustained by your attacker will in all probability cease to exist within a very short space of time. Your injuries could affect you physically or emotionally for life, or the attack could have cost you your life. As I have tried to make clear in earlier chapters, I do not belittle the power and grace of our God to bring restoration into a shattered Christian's life. It is simply that this is not the only aspect we are considering in our discussion about self-defence.

Above all others, your most important asset is your mind. You may have tried a mental trick already in order not to resort to combat (though presumably at this point in time the trick has already failed). Don't stop using your brain just because you have decided to use force. Above all, consciously believe that you can defend yourself. Do not think about how much you may get hurt. Take a positive attitude and look for the right moment to act. The adrenaline build-up in your body will help to sharpen your reactions provided you remain as calm as possible. Once again, never become angry with your attacker. If you do, you risk using more force than necessary, thus reducing the speed of your responses and locking out clear-minded thinking. Some books and one notable television series on self-defence have advocated getting as mad as possible and hitting out with all the anger and hatred you can muster. This is the most ridiculous approach possible—do not do it!

A clear mind is able to see openings for a successful escape, and is of paramount importance in distracting your attacker. When an attacker is facing you, it is not easy for him to know what is going on behind him. The fact is that nothing may be going on, but a well-timed gasp and an open-eyed look to one of his rear quarters will be enough to make him think there is. This unguarded moment in his attack is your cue to defend yourself.

When in a fight you can try to fake an injury to gain an advantage. The story is told of two karate experts who met for a test of skills. One man said before they started, 'Do not believe all that you see.' The contest started and they were almost an equal match. The man who had spoken earlier received a none-too-effective blow and then suddenly fell to the ground and started to roll about crying. His opponent thought that the blow was better than it had seemed even to him, and was concerned about the man's well-being. He crouched over his opponent to see if he could help. Without warning a crushing punch was delivered to his groin. He next remembered waking up and finding a note pinned to his chest. It read, 'I told you not to believe everything!' Of course, there are no guarantees that any particular trick will work, but then again there are no guarantees in self-defence anyway.

Your other assets are the weapons you carry around with you all day. By this I refer to your hands, elbows, head, and legs. There are also weapons of convenience. Included in this category are household and kitchen items, bags, umbrellas, papers and magazines, and just about anything you can lay your hands on. Use your imagination. In the next chapter you will learn how to use some of these 'weapons'. When trying to escape from an enclosed area, throw anything that moves easily at your attacker, including soft things such as cushions and more substantial objects such as chairs or dustbins. Don't forget that the third decision you made was that combat must continue to allow you to escape only. You are not trying to hurt your attacker any more than is absolutely necessary. You are trying to stop him hurting you. There is a world of difference between these two objectives.

If you use a weapon of convenience, such as a brick or rolling-pin, to club your attacker, you should hit him as often as it takes to enable you to escape successfully. You should not continue to beat him to a pulp once he is down and rendered non-aggressive. Using a knife is a little tricky if you don't know how. When first spotting it on a table or work-surface you should lift it so as to keep it hidden from the attacker if at all possible. When using it try to restrict stabs, cuts and slashes to his arms or legs. Never stab the trunk of a body with a knife longer than about 3 inches, except in the most extreme cases of danger, as the stab could be fatal. Most attackers will not like the sight of their own blood and may well decide to find an easier target after receiving quite minor injuries. A useful technique is to make a horizontal slash across the forehead. This area will bleed easily and the blood will get into the attacker's eyes so that he cannot see properly.

It is possible, depending on what you use as a weapon of convenience, that you will have harmed your attacker to the extent that under normal conditions he would require medical attention. He may be unconscious, badly cut, have a broken limb, have sustained burns due to hot liquids or foods, have harmful liquids in his eyes, or grazed eyes. You must escape to a point of safety first, and then telephone the police and an ambulance.

The law and self-defence

In any attempted escape you must keep in mind what the law says. In simple terms, it is that a person has the right to defend himself provided he uses no more force than is reasonable to nullify an attack. The problem remains as to what is reasonable or even necessary, and that will be for a court of law to decide. However, if you can be said to have reasonably believed at the time of the attack that the force you used was necessary, you will be acquitted from any charge your assailant brings against you, on the grounds of self-defence.

If you have taken seriously all that I have said so far in this book, there is every chance that you will remain within the bounds of the law. Essentially you must use your reasonable degree of force to 'nullify' the attack, not nullify it and then create your own onslaught. Nullifying an attack means making it ineffective. If a man throws a punch at you, you are at liberty to evade the fist and either escape or restrain the attacker. You would not be expected, for example, to take hold of a brick and smash it against the attacker's skull several times in succession. If you were attacked by a group of thugs wielding various weapons, you might be justified in laying out each and every one that came in for an attack. In such a situation, with several attackers against one victim, you would quickly become tired and injured if the original number of assailants all remained fit enough to keep coming back for consecutive onslaughts. It would also be obvious that restraint holds on any one attacker would not be a suitable defence. You should continue to defend yourself as necessary until the members of the gang decide to leave you alone.

The degree of force is not always easy to determine. A strong attacker will be angered by an effective but not temporarily disabling defence. You will then be faced with a much more determined and wiser assailant. There are no easy answers here. One thing, however, is sure: it is better to survive an attack and argue about your response afterwards, than not to do enough and get seriously injured or killed. Make sure you write down the sequence of events that occurred as soon as possible. Should a court case be brought by the attacker against you, you will have a clear picture of why you reacted as you did. You will not be able to remember sufficiently well some months after the event, and it will be easier for the prosecution council to convince the court that you overreacted. Do not write your account in an emotional manner. Simply write down the things that were said and the threatening activities that were carried out.

The classification of weapons

In the eyes of the law there are two classes of weapon. One class includes such things as knives and guns. Simply possessing them is sufficient for conviction, and any person found carrying such weapons is liable to arrest. The exception to this is where a licence is held or the carriage is obviously due to occupation or hobby. For example, a butcher carrying home his knives to carve the Sunday lunch is not likely to get arrested, provided he carries them in a safe and discreet manner, such as inside a leather bag. If, however, he carries just one of these knives home in the inside pocket of his jacket, and decides to see a Saturday afternoon football match on the way, he will have a much harder time explaining his actions to the police. I own a full-length Japanese sword and I am not likely to get arrested as I carry it quietly and discreetly to a practice hall. If, however, I carry it uncovered and held in my belt, so that it was ready for drawing and hence use, I could be arrested. A licensed gun owner, such as a farmer, may carry his unloaded weapon to a field, load the gun, and shoot a few rabbits. But he may not carry his gun uncovered and loaded through a pedestrian highway.

The second class of weapon includes just about anything else. The difference is that 'intent of use' must be proven for conviction to occur. For example, a rolling-pin can be put into this class if it is being carried by a person who has definite intentions of using it as a weapon. On the other hand, if you are in the kitchen and a burglar or rapist appears wielding a knife, it can be argued that striking him with a rolling-pin in order to escape is reasonable.

Another type of weapon, called a 'covert' (i.e. secret or disguised) weapon, can be classed as unlawful under given conditions. For example, I personally know how to use a *nunchaku*. This is an Okinawan weapon consisting of two lengths of wood separated by a chain or piece of leather or rope. In the privacy of my home or a training hall, my possession of it is not unlawful. I open myself to prosecution, however, if I carry it with me at all times, concealed about my person, with the primary intention of using it to defend myself. When living in Watford I often saw students of this weapon walking down to the local park, 'playing' with it around their bodies as they searched for somewhere to practise. This is folly to say the least. Any covert weapon should be carried to and from a practice place in such a manner as to make it difficult to bring the weapon into play quickly. If you have to practise in public grounds, make sure you find somewhere very isolated, and stop practising the moment a member of the public is noticed.

I would reiterate one fundamental and important point. Do not use any class of weapon in self-defence unless it is absolutely necessary. However, it is better to use a weapon, survive, and argue the point later, than to be seriously injured or killed. When picking a weapon make sure it is a weapon of convenience and not something you carry about your person 'as a precaution'. In deciding to use a weapon do not bluff. If you are threatening to use it, you must be prepared to do so if necessary. A casual attacker may be put off and leave you alone, but a determined attacker may not be deterred in the slightest.

In conclusion

We have covered a lot of ground in this chapter. Throughout I have tried to emphasize that you are the only one who has to make the final decisions. To help clarify the situation, let us summarize what has been said.

▷ Use preventive measures first.

▷ Accept that you will feel afraid or nervous, but stay calm and composed.

▷ Keep thinking of ways to escape or dissuade your attacker from continuing his intentions.

▷ If forced into a fight:
  – Do not overreact.
  – Believe that you can defend yourself.
  – Remember your aim is to escape only.
  – Do not bluff, make your defence work.
  – Do not use a weapon unless you have to, and then use a weapon of convenience only.
  – Survive first and argue later.
  – Escape to a safe place and then telephone for the police and, if necessary, an ambulance (either for you or your attacker).
  – If your defence caused injury to the attacker, write down what happened. You may need to recall it later on.

By following these guidelines and learning the techniques presented in the next chapter, you will have assimilated the basics of effective self-defence. You will have learned to take precautionary measures wherever possible, and how to escape from an attack should the necessity arise. But there are no guarantees.

Remember that I have endeavoured to supply you with a broad 'family-based' self-defence course. There are three books published in Britain that I would recommend for further reading should you desire it:

▷ *Self-defence, the Essential Handbook* by James Shortt (Sidgwick and Jackson, 1984).

▷ *The Official Self-Defence Handbook* by David Mitchell (Pelham Books (for the Martial Arts Commission), 1985).

▷ *Self-defence for Women* by Paul Redgrave with Carolyn Seaward (Robert Hale, 1983).

These are among the best references for readers in Britain

because they relate to British law. Furthermore, they encourage prevention before physical combat, they shy away from élitist martial arts techniques and stick to what works, and they are the most up to date. Obviously they are not aimed specifically at the Christian reader, so you should absorb only what you find appropriate and useful.

10

Self-Defence Techniques

In the previous chapter we looked at the actions and reactions that form the backcloth to a physical confrontation. Having decided that escape by physical means is necessary, we will hopefully have practised the techniques in this chapter beforehand.

This chapter includes over sixty diagrams, together with suitable comments, to help you perform each technique correctly. Getting your whole body 'behind' any one movement is of vital importance. A single limb movement is not nearly so powerful or effective when the rest of your body takes no real part in the execution. Balance and posture is also primary. When performing a technique, never stretch yourself to the extent where you would lose your balance. Instead, remain within your sphere of balance and move your whole body in the appropriate direction. To enable your body to act as a whole unit, strive to keep your limbs relaxed but not weak. This is difficult to attain without constant practice, but it will improve your technique both in terms of speed and power. If you require undue strength to make a technique 'effective', you are almost certainly doing it incorrectly. Try it again. While remaining relaxed and within your sphere of balance concentrate on circular motion. This motion can be described as three-dimensional or spherical. It can be to the front, rear, either side, upwards or downwards. In other words, to nullify an attack from any direction we should not only stay within our sphere of balance but also move in a spherical manner. Pivoting on one foot while lowering the body is just one example of this. Wherever possible the diagrams include arrows that indicate the circular flow of motion required for maximum effect.

When practising think also of speed and timing. Timing is to do with synchronizing your movements with those of your attacker, while speed is to do with initial evasion and matching your attacker's motion. Strive to be not a split-second in advance of or behind your attacker. In this way you will neither anticipate incorrectly nor react too slowly.

Do not worry if this all seems rather hard to follow. The techniques included in this book have been chosen for their relative simplicity. If you practise them constantly and at least aim towards the well-executed technique, you will do well. Remember that in the street your 'partner' will not be co-operative but probably aggressive. In view of this you would also do well to experiment with the set moves. Make up some of your own by adapting a technique or joining techniques together. Change the angle of attack. Above all, train to remain flexible in your defence. Always practise techniques on both the left and right-hand sides. Once you are in the position of being able to escape from any attack from any direction, without freezing or having to think about motion, you will be much better able to defend yourself.

Awareness

When an experienced driver enters his car he immediately switches to a new mode of awareness. He unconsciously begins to take in a lot more data about his surroundings and what is going on around him and his vehicle. A good footballer will perform a similar switch of mode when stepping onto the turf. How unfortunate it is that most of us switch back to a mode of unawareness so quickly and easily.

The art of self-defence relies to a large extent on awareness. I repeat my previous statement that this is not the same as paranoia. Practise driving long enough and road awareness will become automatic. Practise being aware of your surroundings and possible danger areas at all times of the day, and this too will become automatic.

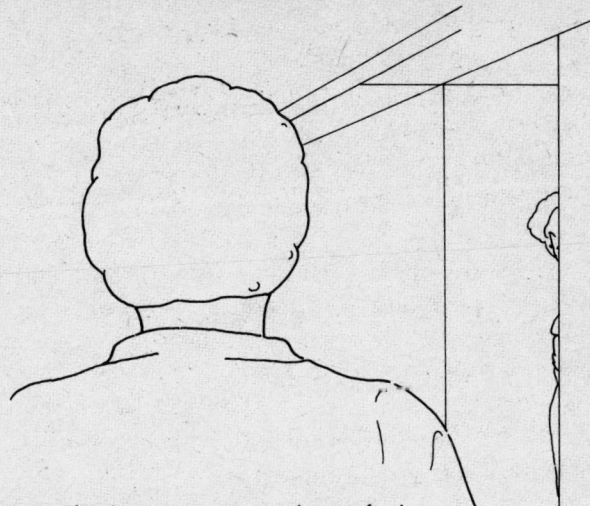

FIG. 1

A major contribution to awareness is to take in as much data through your five senses as possible. By walking on the outside third of a pavement you can see into alleys well in advance.

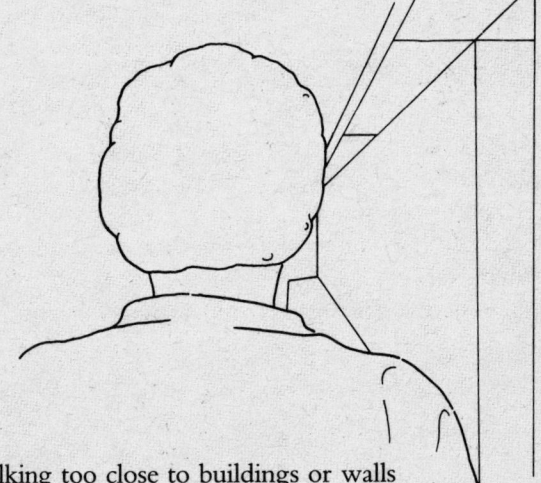

FIG. 2

When walking too close to buildings or walls you open yourself up to more danger. You cannot see so well, you can be easily grabbed, and you have left little distance for reaction time.

Blocking

No amount of training in the world will help you if you end up in a dazed heap on the floor because of a direct hit. Our initial defence will often simply be avoidance, possibly coupled with a block of one sort or another.

The principle of avoidance is easy: get out of the way! We can move to the inside of our attacker or to his outside. Figures 3–6 show the difference between inside and outside movements. Essentially an outside movement is one where we would end up blocking the outside edge of an attacker's arm, and vice versa.

For our blocks to be effective we must remember our circular movements. Either our blocking arm will have some form of curved movement, or our body will move in a partial circle, or both. Common faults are to lean backwards, hence making the block ineffectual, or to reach out forwards and thereby lose balance or miss the attacker's arm completely.

A favourite saying of the Japanese is that in avoiding an attack it is sufficient to move just before an object strikes and just enough to make it miss. With practice you will be able to move quite small distances or turn just a fraction in order to make an attack worthless. Having said this, a timely and effective block (as well as avoidance) is of no small help. Later on we will see how we can progress from a block to an arm-lock or a simple wrist throw.

One last point. When making blocks remember to keep your arm relaxed but not weak. Never aim to catch or grab an attacker's arm, simply move out of the way and block using the underside of your forearm within 6 inches of your wrist.

FIG. 3

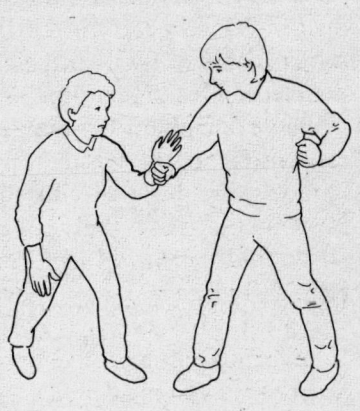

The outside block shown here can be used against direct attacks to the face, chest or abdomen. You can also use it to stop a lapel grab from occurring.

If the attack is from his right hand, you must pivot on your left foot taking your right leg in a circle about 90° to the left. Your left hand, which will perform the block, should be slightly bent.

Keep your hand open, i.e. do not clench it into a fist. If you have time you may find it useful to slide your left foot out to the left before pivoting on it.

FIG. 4

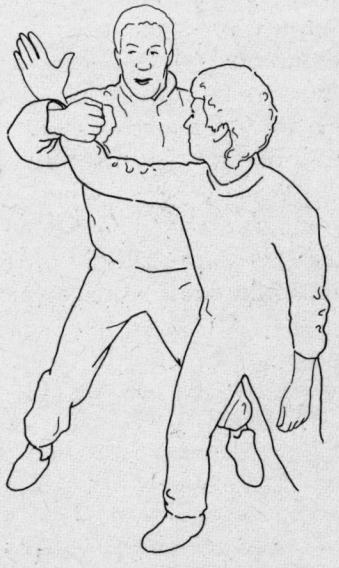

For the inside block refer to figure 4. If the attack is with the right hand, you must pivot on the right foot and block with the right hand.

Notice how open the attacker becomes to counter blows to the groin or face, or simply to being pushed away.

When an attack is more of a 'roundhouse' type blow, it is better to block on the inside of your attacker or block the attack early (see figure 5).

FIG. 5

This is a more direct form of inside block to a 'roundhouse' type attack. For this to be effective you must slide forward and outward on the left foot. Your left hand will come up and move forwards and outwards with your body.

Your weight should be about two thirds on the bent left leg, with the trailing leg left straight. If performed correctly this is an immensely powerful block and could cause your attacker some discomfort and loss of balance. You must block the attack early before it attains full power.

FIG. 6

Strikes made downwards towards your head will normally imply the use of some sort of weapon. An outside block is therefore preferable. The initial moving out and pivoting with the left leg is the same as that described in figure 3.

Using the left hand first and then the right hand, go to meet the descending arm as you pivot. Follow the arm down until your arms are parallel to the floor. Make sure that your arms are straight and that one palm is behind the attacker's elbow.

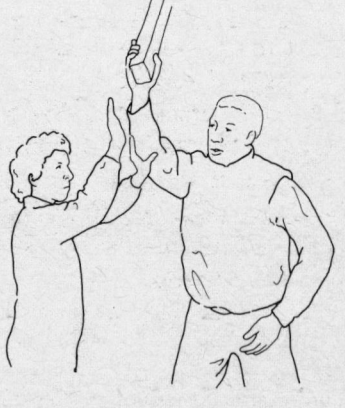

Striking

There are many parts of the human anatomy that, if hit the correct way, will suffer at least some discomfort. If your attacker were to be incapacitated for even a short while, it might give you the time required to escape. Above all, if you decide to strike, you must make it effective. To hit your attacker with no consequential effect is to arouse his anger and place you in even more danger. But never keep striking your attacker out of sheer uncontrolled rage. Remember that to lose mental control is also to lose physical control. Strike if you really have to, strike effectively, and escape.

The strikes included in the following pages are those that have been found to be most easily learned by students on short self-defence courses. You will not become the world's top karate expert, but you will gain some useful armoury. Striking is an art, and there are some general principles within karate that will make your self-defence as effective as your limited training will allow.

The main points are speed, focus, and muscle relaxation and tension. They are all related and must be brought into play in the right order. Wherever the point of impact is to be, that is your focal point. You must focus the energy and power of your whole body at this point and not be distracted in any way. The power of a strike is that which comes from a light object, such as a hand, travelling very fast, rather than a heavy object moving slowly. In the physical sciences the rule 'force = mass × acceleration' is well known. Be fast, be powerful! Also, the shorter the period of contact, the more powerful will be the technique. We have already noted that to move fast means to be relaxed. Only at the moment before impact do you tense your whole body, starting from the abdomen and reaching out to your limbs. In all of this, never forget your sphere of balance.

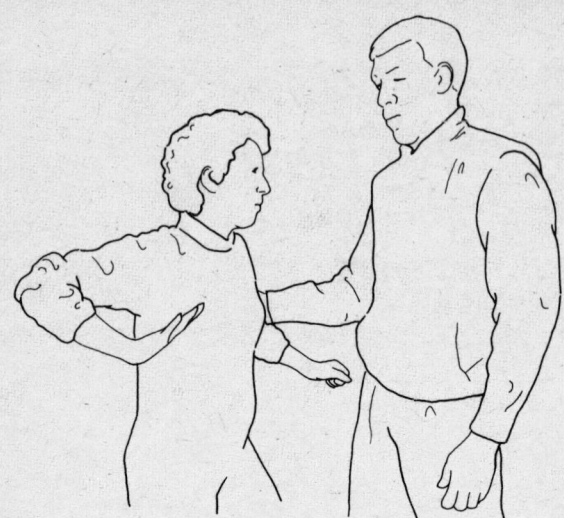

FIG. 7

The palm strike

This is one of the easiest and most powerful strikes possible. Bend your arm back and open the palm of your hand (figure 7). Keep your fingers together and straight. Thrust upwards so that at the point of impact your arm is almost straight and the palm of your hand strikes your attacker's chin.

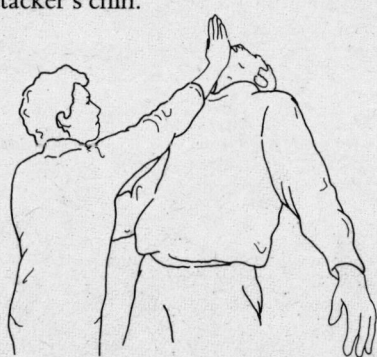

FIG. 8

By the time your arm is fully straight your attacker's head should be pushed back (figure 8). If you move out to the side of your opponent, keep your pushing arm straight, and drive backwards and downwards, your strike will most likely throw him. A palm strike is also effective when applied to the side of your opponent's jaw.

FIG. 9

Heel strike

A good heel strike to the top of your attacker's foot will be about as painful to him as getting shot there, even without pointed heels! If you are not wearing pointed heels, use the back edge of a flat heel. Lift your own foot about 10–12 inches high and then drive down as fast as you can. If you lift your other foot up first, as if you were hopping from one foot to the next, your entire weight could be added to the thrust.

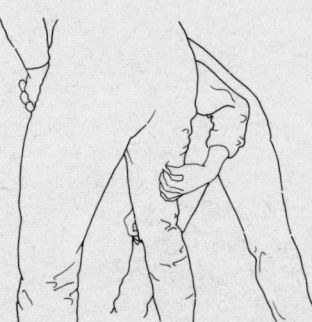

FIG. 10

Rear thigh pinch

If you are ever caught in a head-hold, this technique will soon set you free. Lift your back hand to the rear of your attacker's leg and pinch the soft flesh. This is an extremely sensitive area of the body and the attacker will certainly loosen his grip. Use the surprise nature of the attack to break free.

FIG. 11

Groin attacks

Another very sensitive area of the body. A mere 2 inches to the side and the effect is at least halved (unless your strike is a very powerful one), so aim carefully.

When performing the two-handed punch (figure 11), make sure your fingers are interlocked, the upper joint of your thumbs are pressed against your top (first) finger, and that your thumb ends are bent upwards as far as possible. This gives you a small solid striking implement, with the minimum risk of hurting your thumbs more than your attacker.

Wait until you have your weight on the ground, make the grip described, and thrust forwards and upwards into the groin.

FIG. 12

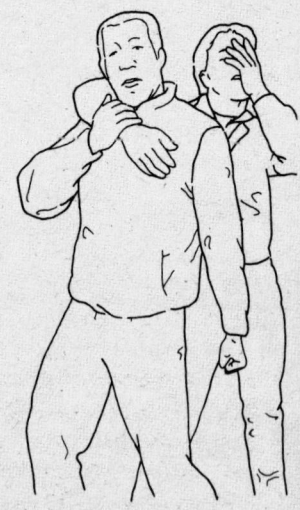

When attacked from behind, a strike to the face (figure 19) followed by a groin strike should give you enough time to escape. In this type of groin strike (figure 12), clench your fist with the thumb on the outside of the fingers. Make the blow by swinging your forearm rapidly from the elbow.

Clearly a front or side kick with your foot could also be applied effectively to the groin area.

FIG. 13

Strike to the solar plexus

If you follow the centre line of your rib cage downwards, you will suddenly come across a very soft spot at the base of the cage known as the solar plexus (figure 13). A strike here will wind your opponent. When striking with your elbow, turn from the hips. Keep your forearm going straight back. Do not let your elbow move outwards away from your body as the strike is made.

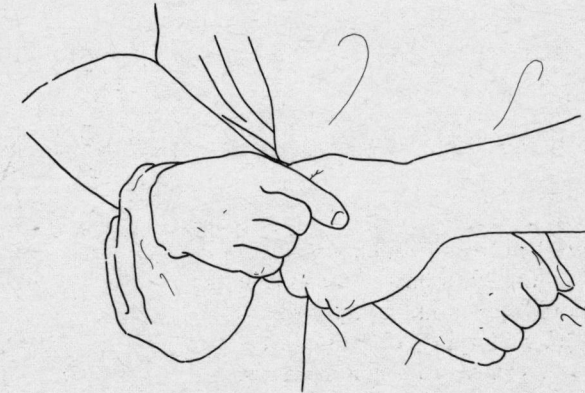

FIG. 14

Pinching the top of a hand

The thin layer of skin on the top of the hand is another good spot for strikes or pinches. You may strike it by clenching your fist and driving in hard with your protruding finger joints (not knuckles). Alternatively you can pinch the skin as shown in figure 14.

FIG. 15

Pushing to the base of the throat

When an attacker is directly in front of you (figure 15), you can push him away by driving your first and middle fingers downwards at 45° into the base of his throat.

FIG. 16

Slapping both sides of the head

A hard slap to both sides of the head simultaneously will be enough to make an attacker loosen his grip. Open your hands, keep your fingers loosely apart, and bring both arms up together. As with any other strike, make the hit with all speed and then withdraw.

FIG. 17

Jaw strike

As well as using the palm strike (figure 8) to attack the jaw, the elbow may be employed. This is most useful when grasped from behind. You will still be able to twist from the waist and you should use this motion to maximum effect when making the strike. Note that in this case (figure 17), your elbow will leave the side of your body in contrast to when hitting the solar plexus (figure 13).

FIG. 18

The nose lever

When an unwelcome arm surrounds your shoulders, or your head is being held (figure 18), putting pressure on the base of your attacker's nose can be very effective. Extend your first finger along the base of his nose and circle upwards and backwards. As he starts to bend over backwards, begin completing your circle by driving downwards.

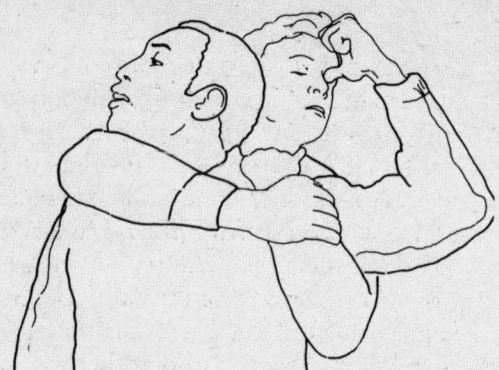

FIG. 19

Eye attacks

The eyes are extremely sensitive and the slightest graze or poke will cause them to start weeping. This will hinder the attacker, first by being painful and secondly because he will not be able to see clearly for a minute or so at least. When attacked from behind (figure 19) you can extend your thumb and use this as a 'poker'. If you are being choked, first turn your head into the bend of the attacker's elbow to enable you to breathe.

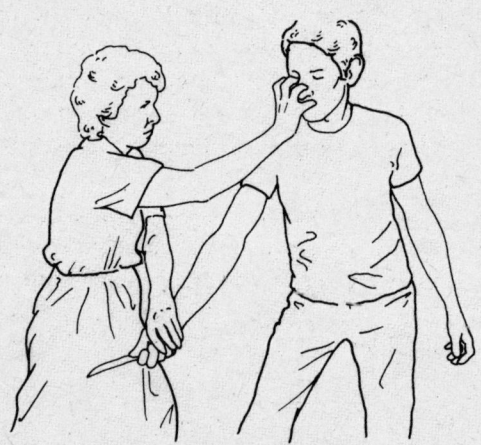

FIG. 20

Many instances could arise where a grazing of your attacker's eyes would not be overreacting. Knife attacks (figure 20) are valid examples. Use the whole of your hand in the shape of a claw and scrape downwards.

Grip releases

It is easier to free yourself from a grip on your wrist or elbow than most people imagine. That is, once you know how. In all grip releases the trick is to apply pressure against the area between your attacker's thumb and first finger. It does not matter, except under extreme conditions, whether there is a noticeable gap or not. So if the thumb and first finger overlap slightly, ignore it. The technique will remain identical.

In breaking the grip you will be moving your wrist or arm in a circle. Imagine a disc, two feet in diameter, vertically in front of you. Your opponent is on the other side of this disc. When starting the technique, turn to face your attacker if you are not already doing so. Your hand will be along the bottom edge of the imaginary disc, gripped by your opponent. To break the grip simply follow the circle given by the circum-ference of the disc, either clockwise or anti-clockwise as follows.

Before making the circular motion, spread your fingers as much as possible. This will help to break the grip by strengthening and enlarging your own wrist. Always move your wrist or arm so that you start going towards the attacker's thumb and first finger. For example, if his left hand grasps your right hand, you will have to circle clockwise. If his right hand grasps your left hand, you will have to move anti-clockwise.

Try to keep your hand in the centre line of your body and twist your hips to accommodate this as you follow the circle. As you finish off the circle you may bring your hand towards your shoulder if it helps. Never curve towards your opponent's shoulder.

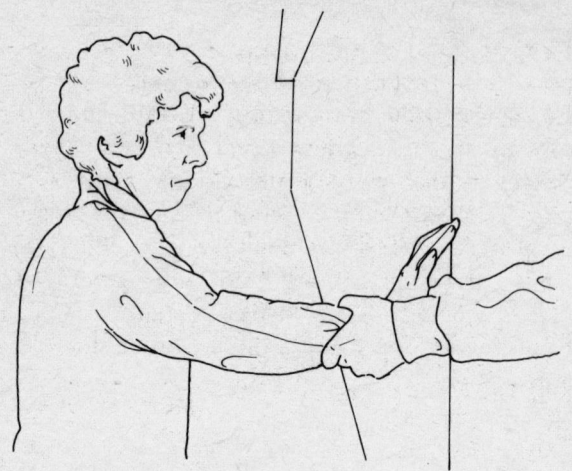

FIG. 21

Figures 21–22 show this circular motion of the wrist. As the two hands pass over the top of the circle the grip is well on the way to being broken. Notice that the fingers are spread. If in figure 22 the woman was to start bringing her hand towards her right shoulder, the grip would be broken completely and with little effort.

FIG. 22

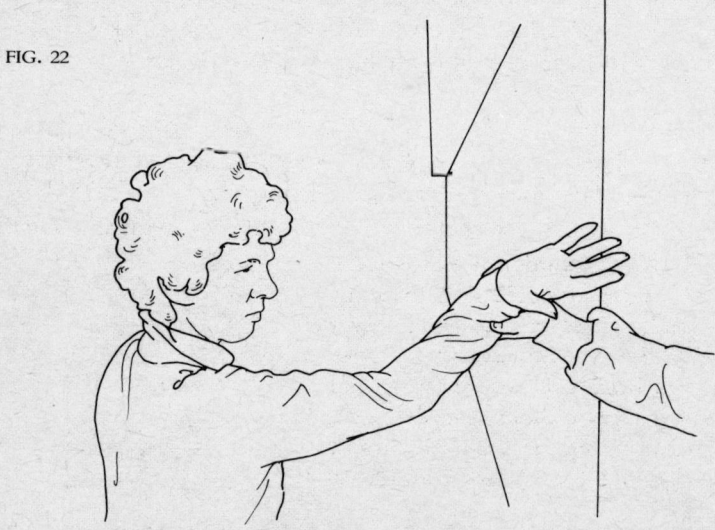

FIG. 23

Grips from the rear are similar to grips from the side or front if only one hand is held. In all such cases you simply turn towards your attacker and perform the technique described above. When both hands are being held from behind a different technique is applicable (figure 23). Assuming both your hands are to your rear, you must slide one foot backwards while bending the opposite knee. This will lower your body while shifting your trunk so that your hands are either beside or in front of you once more.

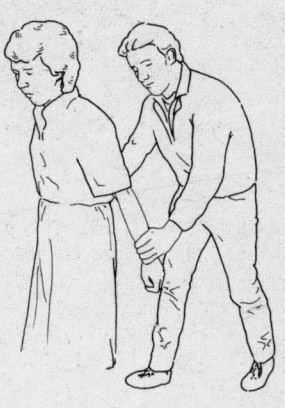

Bending your arms at the elbow only slightly, turn your fingers to the front with your palms uppermost. This action will start to make your opponent lean forwards and lose balance. Not only this, but you will be well on the way to breaking the grip.

FIG. 24

By shuffling forwards and bending the elbows a fraction more, the grip can be completely broken. If you have performed this correctly, your attacker's head will not be far behind your own. If you thought it necessary, this would be a good moment to twist your hips round and perform a strike as in figure 17.

'Pinky' pulling

'Pinky' pulling is polite terminology for wrenching an attacker's little finger backwards against the joint. It is a particularly effective technique, and one that will give your opponent considerable discomfort. Its big advantage is that it is applied against a limb that has very little muscle power in itself to resist. Even people with rather large biceps and chests are open to having their 'pinky' wrenched.

Although angles and grip styles may differ slightly, the 'pinky' pull is one of the simplest techniques to learn. You simply separate your attacker's little finger from the rest of his hand by gripping it with your whole hand, and then pull it back against the knuckle joint.

Figure 25 shows this being performed from a rear clasp around the mouth. As the little finger is pulled back and away from the mouth, you can turn to face your opponent. By keeping the pressure on, it would then be a simple step to dump your attacker on the ground.

FIG. 25

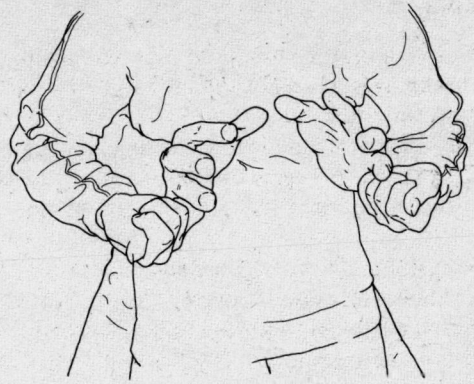

FIG. 26

If an attacker grabs you from behind and lifts you up, there is little point in struggling. It would be better to conserve your strength for when he eventually sets you down again. However, you could still use a 'pinky' technique as shown in figure 26. Separate both his little fingers and pull them backwards and outwards at the same time.

FIG. 27

A similar operation to that shown in figure 26 can be carried out if the grip is applied from the front (figure 27). Once again, separate both little fingers. The only difference is that you will, of course, pull outwards and downwards.

Wrist locks

Included in this section are three ways to manipulate an attacker's wrist in order to throw him away or control him in some manner.

Perhaps one of the most important characteristics of such locks is the way in which you grip with your hand(s). The Japanese use the term *tenouchi*, referring to a grip made with the second, third and little fingers only. Whatever is being held, be it an opponent's hand or a weapon, is forced firmly into the palm of your hand such that there will be no gap between the object grasped and the palm. Your thumb will be used as a light hook or a lever to apply pressure.

All three of the locks shown will inflict severe pain if applied correctly. When practising them, especially in the early stages, never move in a jerky manner or apply excess strength. If your partner says it hurts, believe them. Treat each other with respect and no harm will ensue while training.

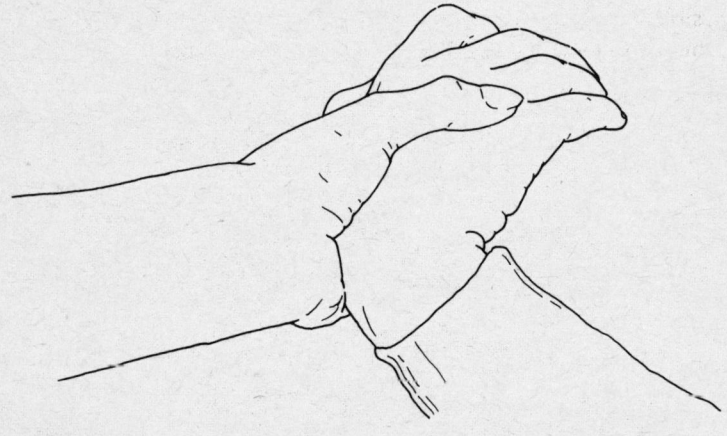

FIG. 28

Figure 28 shows your left hand holding an opponent's right hand. Your fingers should be gripping the underside of his wrist, while your thumb applies outward and downward pressure to the back of his hand. The direction of your push against the wrist is outwards, about 45° to the line of your opponent's forearm. You can easily take your opponent to the floor by circling the hand out and down.

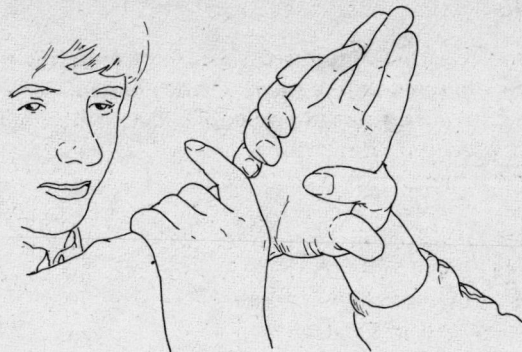

FIG. 29

The lock shown in figure 29 is most effective when your attacker's arm is bent to 90° at the elbow and the wrist. Apply the grip as demonstrated, remembering the point about tenouchi. Circle up towards his face while making his fingers point as near vertical as possible. Continue the circle down towards his stomach—he will be on his knees long before you get there!

FIG. 30

For the technique in figure 30 to work, you must be to the side and behind your attacker. Keep his hand vertical and high enough off the ground to place him on tip-toes. The lock is applied by rotating his hand so that his little finger moves towards his body. The lock is further enhanced by applying pressure against his fingers with your other hand.

Applying basic techniques

Up to this point we have been looking simply at the building blocks of self-defence movements. We will now go on to see how these basic techniques may be applied against both unarmed and armed attackers.

Constant reference will be made to previous diagrams. If you are at all unsure about how to apply a basic lock or break free from a hold, return to the appropriate section and study it carefully. In all areas of specialization, the applied work will never really come to anything if there are no firm foundations. The self-defence techniques that follow are nothing more than examples. The true foundations are laid in knowing the basic moves already covered.

No book in the world will be able to list every defence to every possible attack, least of all when only one chapter is devoted to the subject. Study the basic moves carefully and train yourself to be fluid in thought and reaction. The following examples of techniques will then take their rightful place as springboard training towards the thousands of unrepeatable responses you will naturally make against an equal number of unrepeatable attacks. This is the art of physical self-defence.

Grappling techniques

Under this heading we will be discussing essentially unarmed attacks. Clearly the techniques and forms are equally applicable to armed attacks once you have disarmed the attacker. If you are quick enough, and stay well clear of any weapons, some of the techniques could also be used against an armed opponent.

FIG. 31

Hair pull

Although grips on the hair are painful for most people, the pain is not a paralysing one. Moreover, you are still able to move freely. Ignoring the pain, use this freedom to apply a strike or a lock.

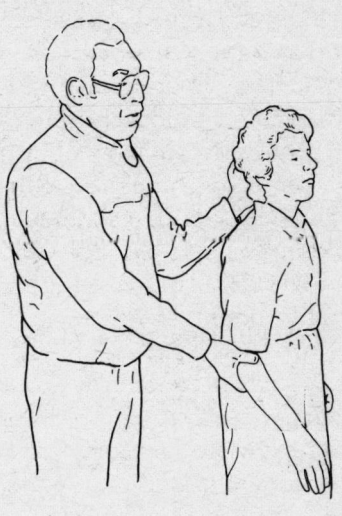

The straight arm-lock shown in figures 31–33 is one example of what can be achieved. Turn into your attacker and raise your inside arm straight up behind the attacker's. In figure 31 the attacker is holding the arm the woman needs to use. By pulling her arm sharply forwards and then sending it backwards and upwards, the grip will be easily broken. The motion will cause your attacker's gripping arm to straighten. This is important for the technique to work.

FIG. 32

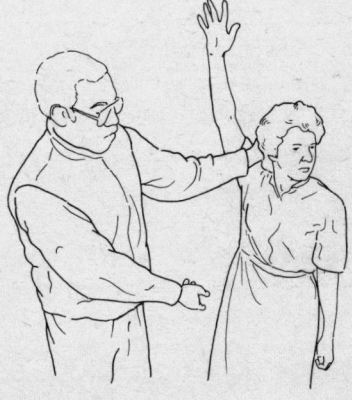

Once you have achieved the position shown in figure 32, there are at least two options open to you. If the attacker's arm remains straight you can apply a straight arm-lock as described in figure 33. If his arm is still bent, move forwards away from him while cutting down against his forearm with yours (or your upper arm just above the elbow). This cutting technique can be seen in figures 35–36.

FIG. 33

Assuming your opponent's arm is straight, start to twist away from him while bringing your arm swiftly down behind his elbow. This will lock his hand behind your head. At the same time apply pressure against his elbow joint. By twisting and lowering (figure 33),
you can drive your attacker to the floor. He will almost certainly release his grip on your hair and then you can escape.

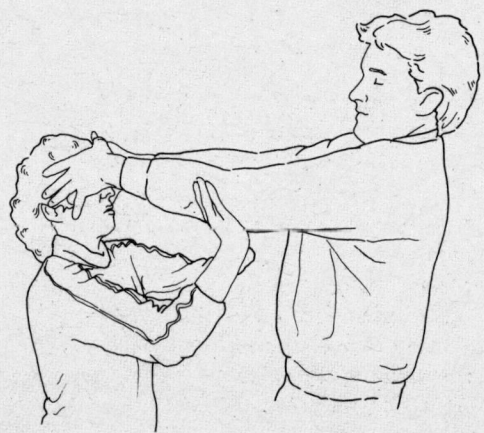

FIG. 34

Front choke

If your attacker has straight arms while pinning you by the throat, you may not be able to apply the strikes described in figures 15–16. An alternative is to place the palms of your hands under his elbows (figure 34). Pushing upwards with your hands will cause him to lose power in his grip. By pushing upwards and forwards you should be able simply to push him away.

FIG. 35

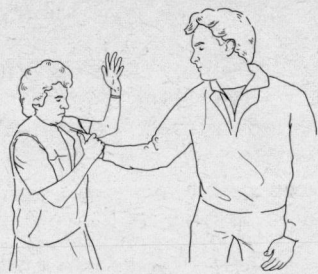

Lapel/shoulder grab

Grabs such as these are usually associated with other objectives such as hitting you with the other hand, head-butting you and so on. You must therefore break the grip while keeping as large a distance from your attacker as possible. Take hold of his fist with your opposite hand and raise your adjacent arm (figure 35). At the same time turn outwards away from him.

FIG. 36

Cut swiftly downwards with your outside arm against his forearm. You can use either your own fore-arm, palm up as in figure 36, or your upper arm just above your elbow. In this latter case your palm will be almost facing you.

At the same time withdraw your rear foot about 6 inches and pivot away from your opponent and downwards. The end result will be to throw your attacker face down onto the ground. You may find it necessary or helpful to drop down onto your inside knee (the one nearest your attacker) at the end of the technique.

FIG. 37

An alternative to throwing your attacker onto his front is to throw him onto his back. Use the same grip as in figure 35, but instead of raising your other arm, grip the attacker's elbow with your thumb uppermost (figure 37). Pivot sideways as before and lift his elbow upwards. By stepping backwards with your inside leg (the leg nearest your opponent) while lowering your body, you can throw him onto his back.

FIG. 38

Pinning with a straight arm-lock

The stance shown in figure 38 follows from the block detailed in figure 6. After you have success-fully blocked down until your arms are parallel to the floor, turn your opponent's arm over and push it downwards. It is important that you hold his arm straight out in front of you (not hugged in), and that your arms are straight.

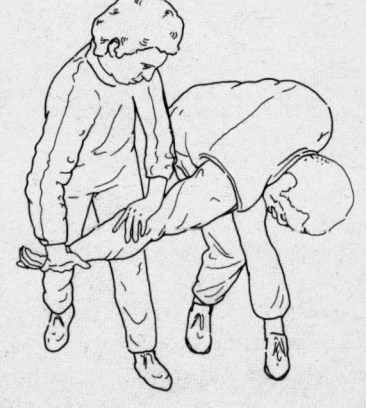

Take two paces forwards while moving your hips in a straight downwards path towards the ground. To pin your attacker down, kneel close to his arm with your outside knee and put pressure on his elbow with your inside knee (figure 39). Do not let go with your hands. Only when your attacker is fully down and obviously held should you attempt to escape.

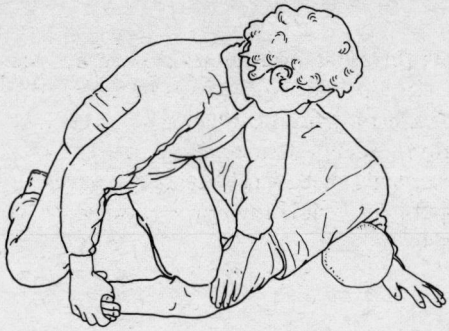

FIG. 39

If your attacker is holding a weapon, it would be wise to get it from him before trying to escape. It is quite possible that he will have dropped it by the end of the technique anyway, but if not you must force the issue. Slide your outside hand down and grip his hand as shown in figure 39. His little finger is near the ground and you are pushing his fingers towards his head. The pressure on his wrist will force him to drop anything he may be holding.

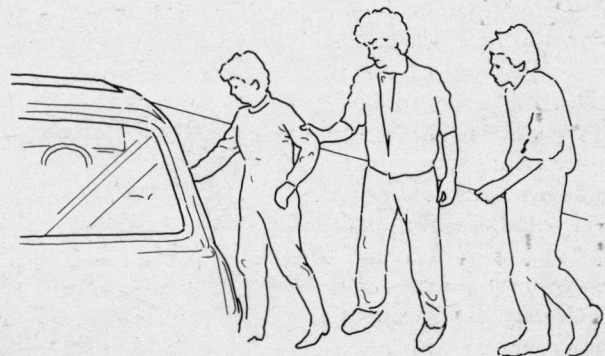

FIG. 40

Multiple attackers

We have already seen how easy it is to break a grip, but this would not be the best thing to do in the situation shown in figure 40. In the case of multiple attackers, the name of the game is to get them in each other's way. By applying an armlock on the first attacker you can break his balance (figure 41). At this instant it would be easy to push the first attacker into the path of the second. Alternatively you could swivel towards the first attacker and immediately apply a palm strike (figure 7). Then deal with the second attacker as appropriate.

FIG. 41

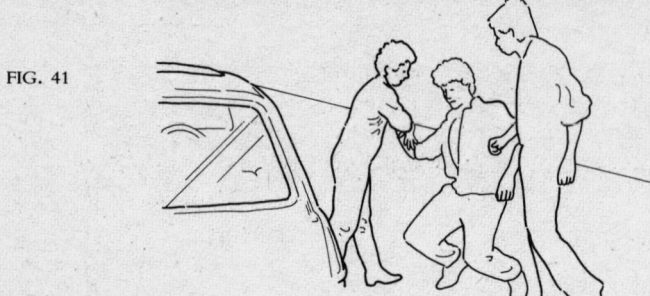

To apply the arm–lock shown in figure 41, swivel towards your
attacker sending your forearm (palm down) underneath his grip.
Bring your hand back so that the hard, little-finger edge of your
wrist makes contact with the top of your attacker's forearm. Hold
your attacker's gripping hand with your free hand. With the hard
edge of your other hand cut his forearm in towards your body and
slightly downwards.

FIG. 42

Using a wrist lock

The wrist lock shown in figure 30
is well suited to unwelcome arms
placed around your shoulders.

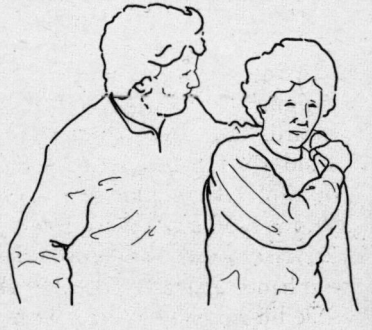

Immediately place your
opposite hand on top of your
attacker's and create the tenouchi
grip. Swivel towards your
attacker, using the power of your
turn to help lift his hand off your
shoulder and over your head.
Leave your hand high enough to
keep him on his toes. Turning the
little finger of his hand in towards
his body (figure 30) will increase
the pain.

FIG. 43

If you now pivot on your inside foot (the foot nearest your opponent) while keeping your hand in the same relative position to your body, you will force your attacker to run in a circle backwards.

By forcing your opponent around in this way you can make sure that you are nearer an escape route than he is before letting go.

If you quickly pull your hand down to the side of your leg while moving him backwards, you will succeed in getting him to his knees. It may be worth doing this before finally letting go.

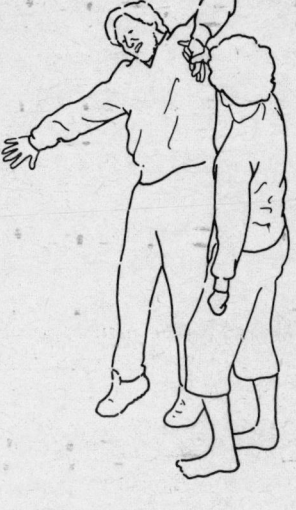

FIG. 44

Escaping while on the ground

In figure 34 we saw that pushing upwards against an opponent's elbows would release the power of a choke grip. Turn the whole thing through 90° and you will start to see a way out of the attack shown in figure 44. By using both hands against an attacker's elbows while hitting his buttocks with a knee, you can throw him completely off you and to one side.

Begin by placing your hands behind his elbows and bending one of your legs (figure 44).

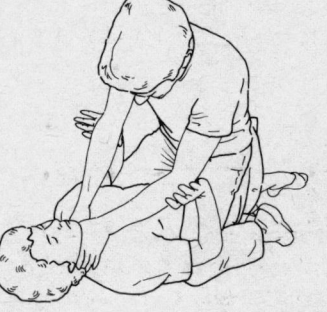

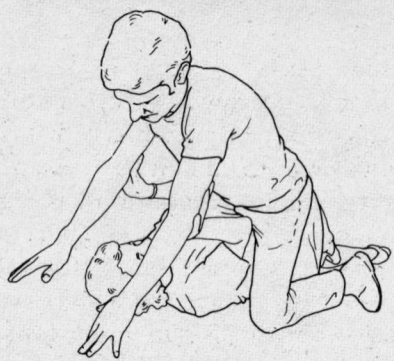

FIG. 45

Move both your hands and your knee away from your attacker's body in readiness to strike fast and hard. Do not move your hands too far away because you do not want to miss his elbows when you do strike. Simultaneously hit his elbows with the palms of your hands and strike him hard in the buttocks with your knee (figure 45). Keep the momentum of your attack going, as if you were attempting a backwards roll.

FIG. 46

As your opponent is thrown clear of your body, twist to one side (figure 46). This will enable you to be completely free from both his arms and his (originally) straddled legs. As soon as you are clear, roll quickly in the opposite direction, stand up and escape.

Knife defence

Defence against any type of weapon is always more tricky than when faced with an unarmed attacker. In the case of knife attacks, there is the constant possibility that you will still receive a cut even though you might have escaped a stabbing. The golden rule when fighting for your life is, 'Ignore bumps, bruises, cuts and blood.'

Figure 61 shows the common stance for a 'professional' gunman. If you were to open his arms wide, drop them down to stomach level, and replace his gun with a knife, you would most likely be looking at a seasoned knife-fighter. It would take an exceptional level of knowledge and skill to defend yourself against such a person. If you are good at running, do that! If you are caught in a trap, I suggest that you do as he says and wait for him to close in and drop his guard or at least give you an opening. Wrapping a jacket or anything else around your forearm could help you ward off jabs and slashes without getting cut. Any weapon of convenience (see chapter 9) that is lying around can also be brought into play.

The techniques shown on the following pages are those to be used against the more standard forms of attack. When practising the moves try to remain conscious of the position of your own body and limbs in relation to the knife. Keep on asking yourself, 'Can I be cut from here?' Always assume that the knife is double edged as this will focus your appraisal more finely. If you feel that your attacker could still cut or stab you, the technique is being applied incorrectly. Finally, always keep the point of the knife away from you.

FIG. 47

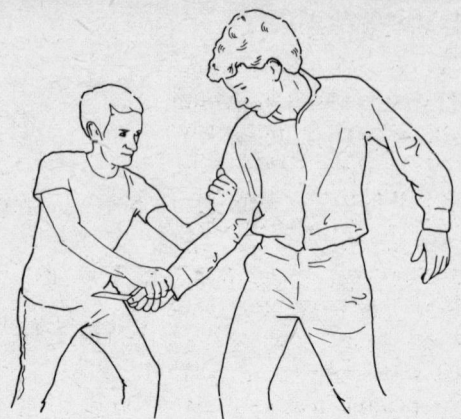

Initial blocks

The blocking techniques described in figures 3–6 are still applicable in armed attacks. When a knife is thrust towards your face, chest or abdomen (figure 47), the outside block shown in figure 3 can be used. Immediately after making the block, grip your opponent's wrist so that you are able to control the movement of the knife.

A downwards thrust with a knife can be blocked as shown in figure 6. Make sure that in following the thrust down you keep one hand behind his elbow and the other hand behind his wrist (figure 48). Once your arms are parallel to the floor, grasp your attacker's wrist as before (figure 47). *Never* try to grab his wrist straight away—you could miss and catch the knife. Block first, then grab.

FIG. 48

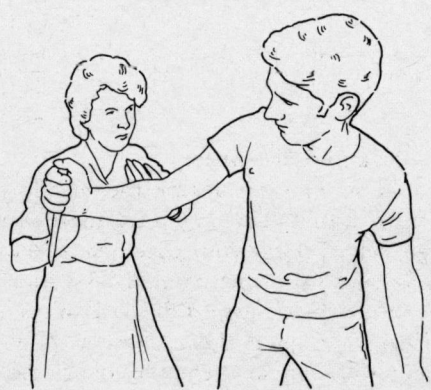

FIG. 49

From either of the above two
blocks, step in towards your
attacker taking your inside arm
over the top of his (figure 49).
Bend your arm back towards you
so that your forearm sits directly
under his elbow joint and your
hand can reach and grasp your
own wrist. Hugging his arm into
your body while pressing
downwards with your hands will
result in a painful arm-lock on
your attacker. You can force him
to drop his weapon and then
throw him backwards by turning
sharply towards him and releasing
his arm at the last moment.

FIG. 50

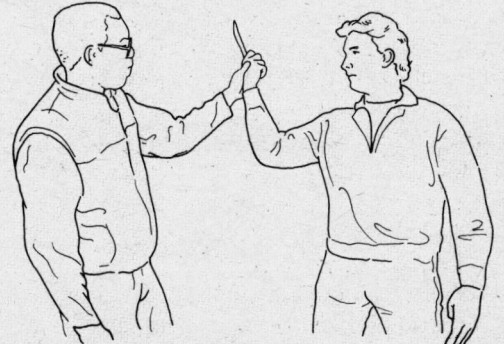

Outside wrist-lock and hold-down

An alternative to the straight arm-lock is the outside wrist-lock (see
figure 28). After successfully blocking in the most appropriate way,
slide the hand currently behind your opponent's elbow or forearm
down to his wrist and grasp his hand. Make sure you take the
correct grip, with your thumb against the back of his hand and your
three smallest fingers gripping the underside of his wrist. Turn
towards your opponent and use the power of this turn to circle his
wrist upwards between the two of you (figure 50). Remember to
keep the blade pointing away from you.

FIG. 51

Continue the circle downwards until your attacker is on the ground and in front of you. Keep the knife pointing away from you and maintain the pressure on your attacker's wrist (figure 51).

Do not bend over unduly in order to keep your grip. If you need to get lower, widen your stance a little and bend the knee of your leg that is nearest his head.

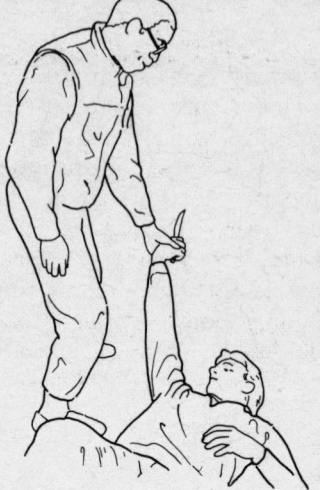

FIG. 52

Reach down with your free hand and take hold of his elbow. Now slide your feet around his head (never cross your feet as in normal walking) while drawing his arm across his face (figure 52).

In doing this you will not only be keeping the pressure on his wrist but also applying an arm-lock on the same arm. As you move around his head in order to turn him over, you should pivot his wrist so that the knife remains pointing away from you.

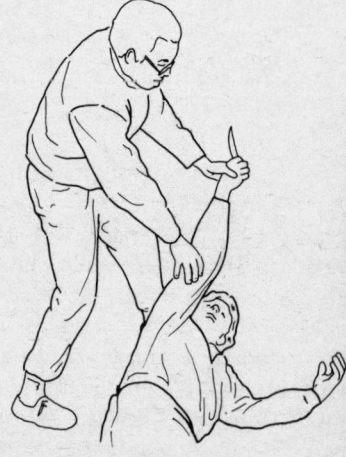

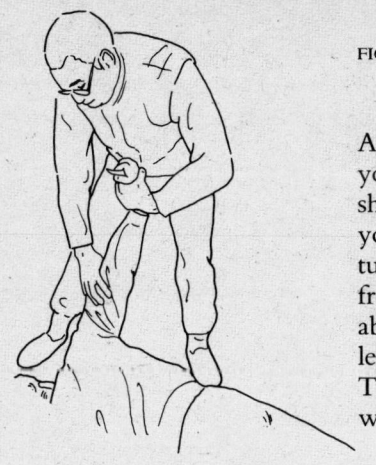

FIG. 53

At the end of the last movement you should be in the position shown in figure 53. Make sure that your opponent is completely turned over and lying flat on his front. Shift your weight so that about two thirds of it is over the leg nearest your attacker's head. This leg should be slightly bent, with your rear leg straight.

FIG. 54

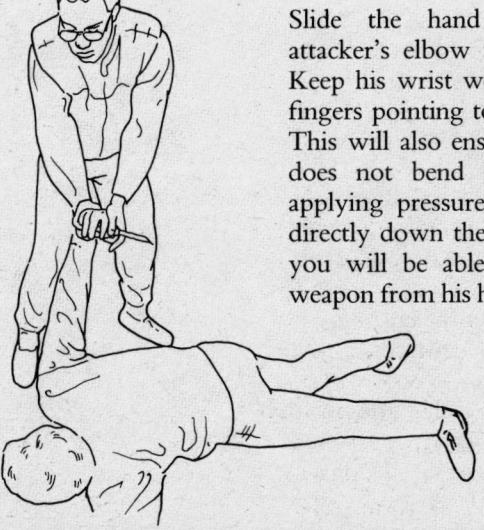

Slide the hand holding your attacker's elbow up to his wrist. Keep his wrist well bent with his fingers pointing towards his head. This will also ensure that his arm does not bend (figure 54). By applying pressure from the wrist directly down the line of his arm, you will be able to remove the weapon from his hand and escape.

FIG. 55

Counter against upward thrust

While an upward thrust with a knife is still in its early stages, it is possible to block the advancing arm and grip the attacker's wrist with both hands. If the thrust is well advanced you would be much wiser simply to step backwards or sideways and wait for a better opportunity to counter.

FIG. 56

When making the initial block, open your fingers and bring your hands together (palms away from you) with your thumbs overlapping the palm and back of the opposite hand respectively. Keep your little fingers and elbows as wide apart as is comfortable. This provides as big a gap as possible for the knife point to move up into. As soon as you have blocked the advance of the attacker's arm, grip his wrist or lower forearm with both hands (figure 55). Immediately step in front of your opponent by lifting his arm over your head and down onto your shoulder (figure 56). Pulling down on the arm with both hands will force your attacker to drop his weapon.

FIG. 57

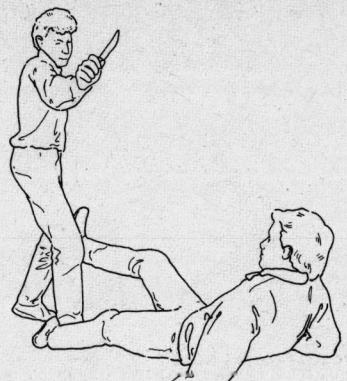

A sacrifice throw

If you find yourself on the ground, either accidentally or because you deliberately fell to avoid an attack, you can still throw your attacker. As he advances, hook one foot behind his front foot (figure 57). Place your other foot either against the inside of his knee or against his knee-cap.

By pulling with your lower foot and pushing (sideways or backwards respectively) with your upper foot, you will successfully topple your attacker (figure 58). If the force of the throw was sufficient, or he lands on a hard surface, you should have enough time to turn away and escape. You will certainly have enough time to get back onto your own feet.

FIG. 58

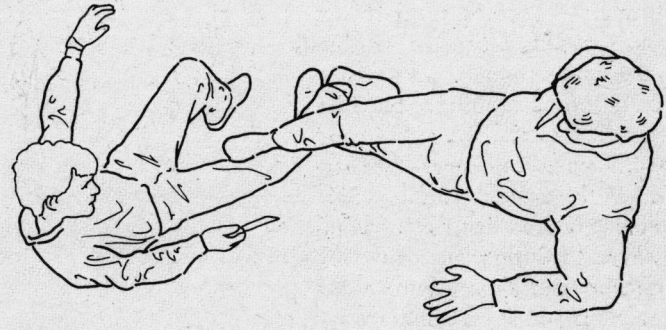

FIG. 59

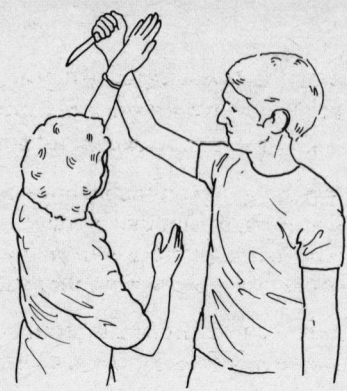

Figure-four armlock

In judo this is known as *ude-garame* and it has many variations. One use for it is in counter–attacking a downward thrust with a weapon. Block the attack with your outside arm. You must do this early, before the attack reaches its full power (figure 59). Your foot movements are as described in figure 5.

FIG. 60

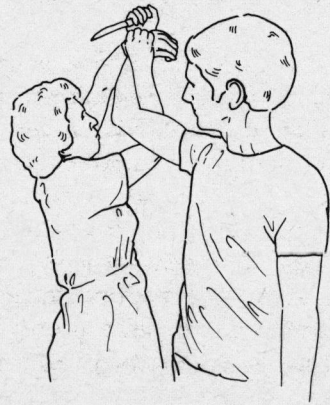

Immediately slide your free arm behind your attacker's upper arm and catch hold of your own wrist (figure 60). Pivot slightly towards your opponent, bending his elbow so that his hand travels towards his shoulder. This will lock his arm tight. Now step forwards and kneel down on your inside knee while keeping your arms at your own chest height. The effect will be to throw your attacker rapidly onto his back.

Gun defence

Defence against a gun is possible under given conditions, but the risks are high. You should certainly never attempt any type of technique unless you are sure about four points:

▷ You are most likely going to be shot anyway.
▷ Someone else is going to be shot anyway.
▷ You can keep the barrel of the gun from pointing at you.
▷ You can get the weapon away from the attacker.

As I have said before, there are no guarantees in self–defence measures. There are even fewer chances of escape if you are faced with a person intent on shooting you.

As with knife–fighters there are two major kinds of gun-man: the 'professional' who really knows how to use his weapon, and the 'mugger' who is less well trained. They are both dangerous. The first is dangerous because he is skilled and will rarely open himself to counter-attack. The second is dangerous because he is unskilled and perhaps nervous. His nervousness could cause him to pull the trigger un-intentionally.

Distance is the main key when dealing with gun attacks. If your attacker is close and has his weapon pressed into your stomach, back or face, you have a reasonable chance of survival. It has been shown time and time again (using blanks) that you can deflect the barrel of a gun enough to cause any bullet to miss you, provided the gun is close to you. You may still get a 'flash burn', but that is hardly the same as getting shot. On the other hand, if your attacker is keeping his distance, never move towards him in order to try and reach him before he shoots. You will never make it.

FIG. 61

The trained gunman

If you are faced with a gunman in this position (figure 61), do exactly as he says.

FIG. 62

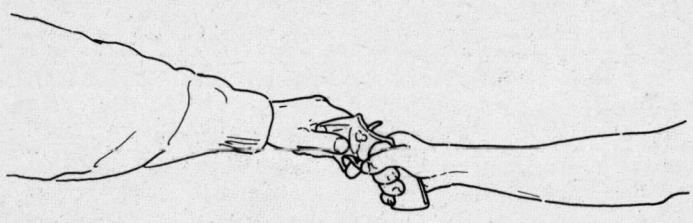

Barrel pistols

The barrel pistol can be halted from being able to fire by gripping the barrel itself (figure 62). By taking the grip shown you could bend the attacker's wrist downwards and outwards in order to break his hold on the gun. Alternatively, you could strike him using one or more of the blows shown in figures 7–20. *Never* try this technique if the hammer of the gun is already back.

FIG. 63

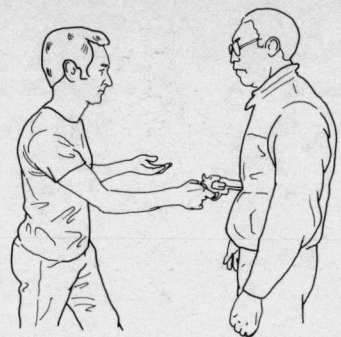

Front attacks

It is possible to strike an attacker's forearm so as to deflect a pistol held at close range (figure 63). The element of surprise is of paramount importance. Appear at all costs to be complying with your attacker's wishes. Start to hand over money or whatever. When his attention is distracted from you momentarily, then is the time to counter.

FIG. 64

Pivot rapidly to the outside of your opponent and at the same time push his arm away from you (figure 64). Grasp his wrist in the manner required for an outside wrist-lock (figure 28). From this position, provided you keep the barrel pointing away from you, you can perform the technique shown in figures 50–54.

FIG. 65

Rear attacks

A similar defence can be used against rear attacks at close quarters. If it is not immediately obvious, turn your head slightly and use peripheral vision to find out which hand the attacker is using to hold the gun (figure 65). Return to face the front immediately. If you are asked to raise your hands, keep them to no more than about head height.

FIG. 66

Quickly pivot to the outside of your opponent, swinging your outside arm down and backwards to deflect the pistol (figure 66). While keeping the pushing pressure against his arm, keep pivoting until you are facing him. With your other hand reach out and take his wrist as in figure 64. Continue your defence as described in figure 64.

In conclusion

I repeat the fact that this book cannot simply be read and then tucked away to collect dust on some old bookshelf. If you want to remain proficient in self-defence, keep coming back to the text. Revise the chapters on preventive defence and child care and practise physical defence constantly with a group of friends. Practising within a group is more beneficial than with just one partner. This is because you will get a chance to try the techniques on people of different sizes and strengths.

Before and after every practice session, perform some warm-up and cool-down exercises as appropriate for your age group. There are many books in libraries that will show you what can be performed sensibly. Overall, the warm-up exercises should include the stretching, twisting and bending of all your limbs. These exercises need not take more than five minutes to perform. Cooling-down exercises should be performed lightly so as to bring your body temperature and heart rate back to normal without causing a stiffening of any muscles. In America self-defence classes are held for pensioners. Some of these people have returned to a class and told how they did manage to protect themselves on a particular occasion. From this we see that anyone can learn at their own level. Physical fitness is of some benefit in self-defence, but it is far from absolutely necessary.

Finally, do treat each other with respect when practising and never fool around within or outside a practice session. Martial arts techniques are far too effective to be played with. If anyone receives a blow accidentally during a session, they should sit down and relax for a short while. Do not repeat the same technique during that particular class. Enjoy yourselves while training, but remember the purpose of it all.

APPENDIX I

A Summary of the Major Martial Arts

There are many different martial arts currently practised in Europe and America. In most cases they will have been imported from Japan, China, or Korea. Some of the arts will be concerned purely with unarmed combat, some with purely armed combat, and some with a mixture of the two.

The diversity of practice within each art makes it impossible to analyse each one, specifying exactly what you might expect to go on in it. In addition, individual club instructors in the less well-known affiliations have a greater degree of autonomy over what they teach and whether or not Zen or some other meditation will be included. This means that although one could almost without fault describe practices within British Judo Association clubs or Shotokan Karate clubs, generalizations would be dangerous.

This appendix, therefore, adopts a very definite form. The major art and sport forms are discussed briefly. Following this there is a short description on how to choose a club. It is hoped that this information will help you to determine the limits beyond which a Christian should not go.

However, before doing this there are two things that should be appreciated. First, as we have already seen, Judo (at least in Britain) is not treated as a martial art. It is an official Olympic sport. You do not, for example, require a Martial Arts Commission licence to practise judo. The British Judo Association will take great exception to anyone saying otherwise. Secondly, very few martial art club instructors 'force' their students to partake in Zen meditation. This is particularly relevant when one realizes that only a very small minority of instructors practise Zen anyway. It is perhaps more common for an instructor to ask his students to sit quietly and concentrate (or 'meditate') on the techniques that they have performed or are going to perform in the lesson. There is a world of difference between these two types of meditation. You would not dream of saying that Bible meditation is evil or bad for you. It is designed to allow you to concentrate on a passage of Scripture, turning it over in your mind again and again, thus becoming more closely acquainted with the meaning and application of the passage. So it is with most 'meditation' in the martial arts. It is a quiet and determined thought process intended to invoke a deeper knowledge or understanding of a particular technique. Treat meditation periods like this and you will never run the risk of compromising your faith.

Of course, if you do come up against a club instructor who is not treating the quiet periods in this way, you will not be able to practise his art. It is simple enough in such a situation to apologize for your ensuing absence and then just leave. In Europe I believe that these instructors would listen to your reason for not wanting to join in such activities and respect your decision. There is little or no basis for the fear that martial arts instructors are ogres never to be crossed in any way. That may have been true in times of old in traditional Eastern training halls, but it is most unlikely in modern-day Europe.

Judo

A sport. No Martial Arts Commission licence is required. The largest body is the British Judo Association. A smaller group is the British Judo Council. Training schedules are nationally recognized. The more lethal moves that exist in other martial arts have been removed. Provided you do not mind getting a few bruises, it is a very good sport to participate in, especially for children and younger people. Competitions are held regularly. Judo is not a self-defence system, though some of the moves could be used in defence. Very popular.

Ju-jutsu

A combative sport and the 'mother' of judo. Retains many lethal moves and is therefore classed as a martial art. Good for self-defence but requires a fair degree of rigorous training. Fairly well distributed throughout the country.

Karate

The Japanese form of 'empty-hand' fighting. It has the largest following of any martial art in Britain. Generally speaking it is a striking art and has no holds, throws or ground restraints. Training is largely geared to stylized movements called *kata*. Competitions are held regularly. Shotokan has by far the biggest following. Other styles are wado ryu, shukokai, shotokai and goju ryu.

Kempo

Three major schools exist for kempo, which is a mixture of striking and grappling techniques. Shorinji kempo is a registered religion and could not possibly be practised by any Christian. Nippon kempo and 'American' kempo are the other styles, and clubs are normally geared towards technique only. Nippon kempo is rather like fancy boxing and protection is normally worn by participants. 'American' kempo is more closely geared towards self-defence measures. Kempo is not largely practised in Britain.

Taekwondo and tang soo doo

Korean forms of karate, often noticeable by their very high kicks. As with karate, they are generally striking arts. Taekwondo is well established in Britain, but tang soo doo is less well known.

Kung fu

The Chinese striking art of self-defence. There are the 'hard' schools that contain powerful kicks as in karate, and also the 'soft' schools that include tai chi chuan. The latter is highly rated by the Chinese, and people of all ages are seen practising it as a form of exercise. Yoga or other Buddhist-type meditation sessions may well be an integral part of the training in both schools. If so, a Christian knows that he cannot take part. Kung fu is fairly well distributed, particularly in the south.

Aikido

There are three main styles: tomiki sport style, the 'soft' traditional aikido schools, and the 'hard' yoshinkan-style schools. The 'soft' schools are proponents of the ki principle to a much larger extent than the other two. If you visit such a school and feel uneasy about the emphasis on ki, you would be unwise to train there. Aikido has a basically passive, defensive character and is well suited to Christian temperament and priorities within self-defence. The 'hard' schools such as British yoshinkan, ken shin kai and shudokan are more closely geared to self-defence than the 'soft' schools. The tomiki style lies somewhere in between the other two, but is more akin to the 'hard' style and commands the largest following.

Hapkido

Hapkido is the Korean equivalent of aikido. It also contains elements similar to judo and karate techniques, and is not dissimilar to ju-jutsu. It is not yet widely established in Britain.

Kendo, jodo and iaido

These three arts are weapons-training in sword fighting, staff fighting and sword drawing and cutting. Kendo is practised with a bamboo sword called a *shinai*, and is the art where you will see heavily armoured practitioners trying to hit each other. It involves rigorous training and is excellent for improving reactions and physical control of the body. Indeed, all the weapons-training arts are geared to personal discipline and improvement rather than to practical self-defence. They are all taught under the auspices of the British Kendo Association which is in turn affiliated to the Martial Arts Commission. Jodo is usually practised in pairs, with one person using a wooden sword called a *bokken* and the other a *jo*. Iaido is practised alone and with a sheathed metal sword. These arts are gaining in popularity as the facilities and opportunities for training improve.

Adopting one of the arts

I believe that if you have read this book carefully, you will already know what to look for in a club. However, for the sake of clarity and security let us review the situation once more.

If you wish to learn simple self-defence, your best move is to contact a local college or library to see if there are any such courses currently being offered. If not, you will have to seek out a martial arts club of some sort. Do remember, though, that most clubs do not exist to teach you self-defence but an art form. If all else fails, use this book and any others suggested to practise with a friend at home. Any good self-defence course will include talks or notes on crime prevention and general awareness. If a course is aimed purely at the physical side of things and limited to the techniques of just one art, it is performing a great disservice to the public and is unlikely to be that useful to you.

If you do want to learn an art with all its intricate details, the study will reap much reward—but not overnight. Choose the sort of art you would like to learn and visit as many different clubs and styles as possible before deciding. If the club seems friendly, the instructor is well qualified and no philosophical meditation is required, why not have a go? Some Christians I have spoken to say that they could never practise a karate form because it seems to instil too much aggression in its practitioners. A similar argument is sometimes aimed at ju-jutsu. I would rather like to think that this was simply due to the clubs that these people visited. There are good and bad karate clubs, good and bad aikido clubs and so on.

Any martial arts club should be able to instil more confidence into you and prepare you physically and mentally for self-defence without making you a more aggressive person. In fact, the opposite should be true—you should start to become more placid and less aggressive. If after a year of training this does not appear to be happening, perhaps you should stop training in that particular art.

Finally, don't forget about the Christians in Sport Martial Arts Fellowship (CISMAF; see appendix 3). Whenever possible, this group will put you in contact with a Christian instructor in your area. CISMAF may also be able to supply you with precise and up to date details regarding the terminology and practice activities of particular arts. Such information will have been compiled by a leading Christian exponent in that art. The group also displays notice of all its seminars through leading Christian magazines.

The Martial Arts Commission

The Martial Arts Commission is the governing body of all martial arts in Britain. It was set up in 1977 in answer to requests by various government and sports bodies to bring the arts under some form of authenticating control. The major aim was to promote the competent and officially graded instructors and their clubs, setting them apart from the many unqualified 'teachers' that were springing up all over the country.

There is good reason to use membership of the Martial Arts Commission as a yardstick. MAC membership has risen by at least six-fold in just under ten years, giving 1986 totals of around 100,000 practitioners and more than 4,000 clubs. British martial arts are also well respected, and deservedly so, in the Eastern countries.

When looking for a club to train at, do check to see if the club instructor and his students are members of the Martial Arts Commission. This is assuming, of course, that you are not considering judo. As mentioned, the test is not foolproof, but it is at least an attempt at checking for reasonable qualifications.

APPENDIX 2
Japanese Historical Periods

A summary of Japanese historical periods together with some cultural notes relating to both religion and the martial arts is given below. All dates are after the birth of Christ. Note that the Shinto religion existed in Japan before Buddhism officially arrived. Feudal and other national wars were in existence before the formal rise of the warrior class near the arrival of the Kamakura period (c. 1185).

552   Buddhism officially introduced to Japan. Speculative form emphasizing concept of 'nirvana' (non-being).

Nara period 710–794

729–749   Great era of Buddhist idol manufacture (Tempyo period)

Heian period 794–1185

805   Monk named Saicho introduces Tendai sect. Had a practical (works) approach to a person's spirit reaching paradise or being sent to hell.

806   Monk named Kukai introduces Shingon sect with gnostic emphasis.

1175   Founding of the Jodo sect. Repetition of the sacred formula 'Namu Amida Butsu', calling upon the compassionate Buddha, was sufficient for salvation. Hence a religion of faith alone without works.

1180–1185 Gempei wars. Start of the rise of the warrior class. The Japanese sword became worshipped and honoured. On making a sword a smith would purify himself under Shinto (not Buddhist) rites.

Kamakura period 1185–1336

1191   Introduction of Zen (Rinzai) sect. A road to enlightenment through discipline and inner control. As Shinto had so little to offer, any warrior who was in any way religiously inclined had very little choice but to follow a Buddhist sect.

1192   Yoritomo becomes Shogun. His power was based on the new warrior class, the samurai.

Ashikaga period 1336–1573

1336–1392 Nambokucho period. Continuous struggles.

1392–1573 Muromachi period. Struggles continue. In 1534 there started the Sengoku-Jidai period where the whole country was at war. This lasted until the year 1615. In 1549 the Jesuit missionary Francis Xavier landed and began his work. The Japanese admired Jesuits because they exhibited a discipline similar to that of the best Zen monks. Devotion to a lord was absolute, and the Japanese also understood this well. The Ashikaga Shogunate terminated in 1573.

1582   Jesuit Visitor-General reports to Rome that there are 150,000 Christians and 200 churches in Japan. A good many samurai and some daimyo were among the converts. They wore crosses on their helmets when entering into battle. Many remained faithful to their vows through the severe persecution that was soon to come.

1587   Christian missionaries and Christianity banned (thought to be due to pressure from Buddhists and a possible small-time slave trade). Most missionaries left but some remained and worked underground.

1596   Total number of Christians considered to be around 300,000.

1614   Ieyasu issues an edict suppressing Christianity.

Tokugawa period 1615–1867

1615   Japan free from civil war. Samurai concerned with administration. Martial arts still practised, now also refined and categorized.

1622–1638 Period of greatest Christian persecution. Tens of thousands were slaughtered. Christianity was forced to go underground.

1783 Rice riots start. Shogunate opposed.

1838 Famines. Shogunate embarrassed.

Meiji period 1868–1912

1868 Shogunate overthrown. Power restored to Emperor. Emperor's Charter Oath. Edo (Tokyo) established as the new capital. Japan emerges from feudal period. Country opened to foreigners. Christian families were discovered who had passed on their faith in secret from father to son over a period of more than two centuries.

The term 'jutsu' became 'do' (e.g. kenjutsu became kendo). Martial arts (now 'ways') practised more for philosophical benefit.

1873 End of ban on Christianity.

1876 Samurai banned from carrying swords.

Taisho Emperor 1912–1926

1914 Japanese declaration of war on Germany (World War I).

1920 Peace concluded with Germany.

1921 Formation of Japanese Communist Party.

Showa Emperor 1926–

1939 Outbreak of World War II in Europe.

1941 Attack by Japanese on Pearl Harbour. Start of Pacific War.

1945 Atomic bombs used on Nagasaki and Hiroshima. End of World War II.

1956 Japan admitted to United Nations.

APPENDIX 3

Christians in Sport and the Martial Arts

Christians in Sport (CIS) is formally a charitable trust. It became registered in 1980 after a number of years of informal ministry to sports personnel. One of its major aims is to encourage the appointment of local ministers as chaplains to professional football, rugby and cricket teams. Local fellowship and prayer groups, conferences and links with universities and colleges are also part of the work.

CIS has a Director (the Rev. Andrew Wingfield Digby), a National Executive Committee (that includes Gerald Williams and John Boyers) and a Council of Reference (that includes the Rev. Gilbert Kirby, Cliff Richard and Edward P. Waxer (USA)). The main goal is to support Christians actively engaged in the world of sport and bring the good news of Jesus Christ to those sports people who have not yet heard it.

CIS also acts as an umbrella organization to special interest groups. For martial artists there is a group called the Christians in Sport Martial Arts Fellowship (CISMAF). This group aims to act as a central point of reference for both active martial artists (at all levels) and Christians wishing to learn either self-defence or a martial art.

CISMAF has the following major objectives:

(1) To provide a central register of British and international exponents at all levels. This would be used as a contact file for the benefit of Christians in any locality, and also as a dissemination list for information on seminars etc.

(2) To organize and run seminars, conferences and short courses for martial artists of all types. The purpose of such activities would be to pool resources of knowledge and share skills.

(3) To use the register and organized courses as a means of generating localized fellowship groups, with members dedicated to praying for one another and meeting one another's needs.

(4) To further support local CISMAF groups in their endeavours to share their faith in Jesus Christ within the world of the martial artist.

If you are an exponent at any level or are simply interested in practising a martial art or self-defence and you would like to know more about CISMAF, please send a stamped addressed envelope to The Secretary (Dept. CISMAF), c/o Christians in Sport, P.O. Box 93, Oxford OX1 1QX (tel. 0865 240407).